120 Difficult Conversations to Have With Employees

How a Manager Should Discuss Performance, Inappropriate Conduct, and Common Work Situations

By: Dave Young

Table of Contents

Introduction

The purpose of this book is to provide managers and supervisors with a resource to assist them in conversations that are difficult or uncomfortable to have with employees. The topics are divided into 14 sections and there are 120 situations covered in total. The book is written using a question-and-answer format, so it is easy to read and follow. Each topic is covered in two pages, which makes for a quick read.

The book is very clearly laid out and easy to read. It is written concisely, and the topics are clearly defined. The book would be a good resource for a manager to use when struggling with how to approach certain situations. The book gives guidance on what to say and provides examples of questions that can be used in the conversation.

The book tells you about 120 different situations and how to deal with them. It tells you about the right time to take action, what to say in such situations, and why you must have these conversations with your employees properly.

This book can be used by both employers and employees alike. The idea behind this book is that the employees should feel comfortable if they ever have any problems or concerns regarding their job or their employer. This way they will feel more open to speaking up about what is bothering them at work.

You can learn from the different stories in this book about how you can handle these situations in a better way, and make sure that it does not affect your relationship with your employees in any negative way.

The book also tells you to not let these difficult conversations affect your relationship with your employees, because this will lead to a lack of communication which, in turn, will lead to more problems down the road.

Having these difficult conversations allows you to understand each other better which helps keep the relations positive between ourselves and our workers, as well as between ourselves and the other people working in the same field/company. The discussions also help you understand the values and principles that are important to employees which can help with the level of trust between you and them.

The book is organized into different topics such as Performance Issues, Policy Violations, Termination, and other important issues, which makes it easier to find the topic you are looking for. The advice given in this book is applicable for both employees who want to speak up, and for the employers who want to make sure that they communicate better with their employees.

The chapters end with a recap where I try to sum up what was discussed in that specific chapter. You can also look at the common phrases used in these difficult conversations and how they are used in a better way, so that you can use them when needed.

I will help you understand how you can deal with different situations at work more effectively. You should know how to deal with difficult conversations because it helps build positive relationships with your workers without letting such conversations affect your relationship with each other.

Sometimes people feel like they don't have any problems at work, but even then, it's a good idea to read this book because by reading it you will learn how you should approach your worker if you ever do have a problem with them.

I would recommend this book to anyone who is looking to learn more about how to deal with difficult conversations. As stated, this book can be helpful for employees as well as employers. The book will help you understand how you should deal with your workers and how they should deal with you to have a better relationship with each other.

I hope that you enjoy reading this book as much as I enjoyed writing it.

Preface

If you were given a chance to learn how to handle difficult conversations, wouldn't you grab that opportunity? *120 Difficult Conversations to Have with Employees* offers a good way for you to learn how to handle such situations.

This book is short and easy to read. It has 120 scenarios, and it is presented straightforwardly. The book is not a theoretical manual as such, but it instructs you on how you can effectively deal with your employees.

This book contains stories of different people, like managers, CEOs, HR consultants, and other workers who have faced situations where they had to have difficult conversations with their employees.

The scenario stories are quite fun to read and situational based, too, which makes them easy for you to relate to your problems and situations. You can use these stories as examples from which you can also learn something new about handling such situations in a better way.

These different cases are followed by my opinion on them, which gives you an idea of what should be done in each specific situation. In each case, I will also share my personal experience regarding that specific topic which makes it easier for you to understand the topic from my perspective, too.

Fraud

Fraud is the act of deceiving someone to get some advantage or make a profit. Fraud is the most common crime committed by employees, according to the Federal Bureau of Investigation (FBI). The FBI's Uniform Crime Report for 2016 reported that there were more than 1.5 million cases of fraud committed by employees in the United States.

It is estimated that the cost of fraud committed by employees is approximately $300 billion per year. The FBI reports that there are approximately 1,500 white-collar crime investigations initiated by the FBI each week. Approximately 25% of these cases involve some type of employee misconduct and/or fraud.

Fraud can take many forms, including:

- Embezzlement (fraudulently taking company funds for personal use)
- Conflicts of interest (using your position to help a friend or family member gain a business advantage over your employer)
- Forgery (altering a document)
- Bribery (offering or accepting money in exchange for influence or favorable treatment about an official action)
- Larceny (taking money or property that does not belong to you)
- Conspiracy (agreeing with someone else to commit a crime, such as fraud)
- Computer-related fraud (using computers to commit a crime)
- Theft of company merchandise or property

In addition to the financial cost , there are other costs associated with employee fraud. These include:

Lost Time Due to Investigation and Resolution of Fraud Allegations

Fraud investigations can be complex and require significant amounts of time and effort. This is true regardless of whether the allegations are accurate or false.

Also, whether an employee is terminated due to fraud or for other reasons, the time required to resolve the issues often cost employers far more time and money than if an employee was terminated for cause.

In some cases, employees who have been terminated for committing fraud may file a lawsuit against their employers for wrongful termination.

Lengthy Resolution Process

Suits alleging wrongful termination can take years to resolve and can be very costly for employers.

Also, if an employee who has committed fraud, takes trade secrets or other confidential information from a former employer, and uses it in his/her new business venture, that business may suffer competitive harm because the information belongs to another employer that does not want it to be made public.

Emotional Cost

Employees who cheat their employers can hurt the employer's reputation and integrity. Also, when employees cheat their employers, they may put the company at risk of being exposed to additional fraud because the employee who committed fraud may have been working with someone else who may continue to perpetrate fraud even after the first employee is terminated.

Lawsuits

Employers that terminate employees for committing fraud risk lawsuits from those employees for wrongful termination. If an employee successfully sues for wrongful termination, an employer may be required to pay damages or reinstate the terminated employee in addition to paying legal fees it incurred defending itself against a lawsuit.

Without further discussion, let's take a look at some of the common issues that involve fraud in the workplace and how you can handle these difficult situations when they do happen.

1. Fraudulent Expenses

Fraudulent expenses are a difficult conversation because they violate the employer's trust and could be construed as theft.

Best Approach

A manager must treat this situation with tact and must not overreact.

Fraudulent expenses should never be a surprise. If a manager has been lax in monitoring expense reports, the situation is even more difficult. The manager should get advice from Human Resources or the Employee Assistance Program before talking to an employee.

It's rare, but it is possible that something has occurred. The manager may never know which is true if he or she asks leading questions, and the employee will be justifiably offended if the manager treats him or her like a criminal.

A manager must emphasize that expense reports represent commitments to the company to keep accurate records. Requiring an employee to reimburse for expenses that were not allowable is not punishment, but rather an opportunity to learn from a mistake and reform behavior.

When to Approach

A manager should have this conversation as soon as possible after the alleged incident. The longer that it takes to have this conversation, the more difficult the situation becomes. There are many reasons why it may take a long time before a manager can talk with an employee about this issue.

Final Tips

It can be easy for a manager to get angry or upset when talking about these types of situations. This is normal, and it will help the manager to have prepared ahead of time so that he or she knows the facts and all the relevant rules regarding expense reimbursement.

A manager should avoid asking for reimbursements from employees in these situations unless he or she has the appropriate receipts. It is very easy to forget to ask for receipts, but it can be devastating if a manager asks an employee for proof of reimbursement and then does not get it.

A manager should never accuse fraud without knowing all the facts. All of the facts are not known until an employee admits that he or she has done something improper or until a manager has seen receipts and other supporting documentation.

2. Suspected Theft

The main concern of any business or organization is the security of its assets. Theft is a serious offense. The company must ensure that the right people work for it, and they are properly motivated to deliver the best results. It is thus essential that proper checks are put in place to identify dishonest employees and remove them from the workforce.

Best Approach

To have a conversation about theft, you should be well prepared. It is not enough that you know that an employee in your organization is stealing from work or the company. You must have proof to back up your accusation and the conversation.

The best approach is to use reverse mentoring techniques. This means that you will sit down with the employee and ask them what they think you are investigating them for. If you can build some trust, they may be more likely to confess or at least give a hint as to what it is that they may have done wrong.

However, you should be careful if this is a case of office politics, and one of your seniors may be behind the allegations.

If there is any evidence of theft, you must ensure that it is collected and presented in a neat file with copies of all relevant documents. You must also present this file as if it were part of an investigation by Human Resources or law enforcement agencies (if there was an internal investigation).

The conversation should be short, direct, and professional but respectful at the same time. You should explain why this has come up and why it could affect their future relationship with the company.

There should not be any room for misinterpretation or false accusations. You might want to consult a Human Resources specialist to prepare for this conversation or help you with it.

When to Approach

Once you have proof that there is a possibility of theft in your organization, it is best to approach the staff member who has been accused of stealing. Ideally, you want to talk to him or her as soon as possible. You want this conversation to come from the top down, but it is also essential that you deliver your message with tact and empathy. You must be careful not to accuse the employee of stealing or insinuate that they have stolen from the company.

What to Say

"I'm calling you in today because we have discovered that there is a possibility that one of our employees has been stealing from the company. I don't know if this is true or not. I do not want to make any accusations, but I do believe that the best way for us to resolve this matter is for you to tell me what you know about it. I will not judge you, and we will deal with this matter discreetly and confidentially."

Final Tips

Always be calm and collected during the conversation. There should not be any sign of anger or frustration. Avoid blaming the employee for what he/she has done wrong. You should indicate that it is not their fault but the responsibility of the entire organization. This will also ensure that they do not feel isolated. This might lead them to further criminal activities.

Do not forget to have a witness present. This will help you maintain your objectivity and keep the situation under control.

If you have any evidence of theft, make sure you present it professionally. You should avoid being confrontational or aggressive during the conversation. The employee will be less likely to feel threatened and more likely to open up to you if they are not on the defensive.

The conversation about theft must be as honest and direct as possible. The employee might deny the charges, but you must have a valid reason to suspect them and the evidence to back your claim.

3. Vendor Invoicing Fraud

One of the easiest ways to embezzle funds from a company is through vendor invoicing. A vendor invoice is a document that allows a company to pay a supplier directly without going through the official funds' transfer protocol. It's relatively easy for an employee to request an invoice from their favorite supplier and then deposit it into their bank account.

Best Approach

This is a difficult conversation to have with an employee because it means that you must confront them about something that they may not even be aware of. They are likely to feel embarrassed and defensive, possibly even angry, and they may feel like you are accusing them of wrongdoing.

It's also important to explain why it's necessary to investigate an employee for this type of embezzlement. Even if their actions have resulted in no loss for the company yet, they still need to know that you aren't going to tolerate fraud and dishonesty in any form — which will send a clear message about your standards.

If there has been any loss, and it is a relatively small amount, you may decide to take no further action. If there hasn't been any loss, you should ask the employee to pay back the money immediately and explain that you would like them to reimburse your company for the interest that is payable on late payments.

Finally, if they have stolen company property or equipment, you may need to either seek compensation from them or add this cost to your annual accounts as an intangible asset.

When to Approach

If you have a concern that your employee may be involved in vendor invoicing fraud, you must address this as soon as possible. If you wait for several months before investigating it, the employee may have already embezzled a significant amount of money from your company.

What to Say

"There has been a discrepancy between the invoices approved by accounts payable and what was paid. You have issued several invoices to vendors recently, and I have concerns that you may be involved in vendor invoice fraud. There has also been a loss on one of these transactions. I need to ask you some questions about how many invoices you have issued over the last few months, and I would like to see copies of all these invoices."

Final Tips

It's important not to jump to conclusions in this situation, and not to accuse the employee of any wrongdoing until you have proof. It's also important not to make any accusations until you have discussed the matter with another senior member of staff such as an accountant or financial officer.

You should also make sure that you have a clear policy in place which states the rules regarding vendor invoicing. This should be discussed with all employees during their induction process and updated regularly to ensure that the policy is up to date.

4. Overcharging the Company

Have you ever had to confront one of your employees for overcharging the company on an expense report? I know I have. This is one of the more difficult conversations to have with an employee. It is an awkward situation where you are questioning their integrity and trustworthiness.

Best Approach

I believe the best approach when confronted with an employee who is overcharging expenses is to keep a level head. You are not going to get anywhere by screaming at someone for overcharging the company.

I recommend bringing them into your office and sitting down with them in a private environment. I believe it is important that this meeting is held in private and not in front of others. As far as you are concerned, this conversation is about finding out how the company can resolve this issue and not so much about pointing fingers at an employee.

Explain the facts to them, including any documentation you have found that confirms your suspicions; then ask them if they have any idea how it could have happened, because you don't want to accuse anyone of anything without knowing all of the facts first. I always like to first find out if someone is willing to take responsibility for their mistake before I begin accusing them, because sometimes mistakes can happen without malice involved.

Don't be surprised if your employee becomes defensive during this conversation. If they do become defensive, you will have to regain control of the situation before they walk out of the room. You can regain control of the situation by telling them that this is not about judging them or placing blame; rather, it is about working together to solve the problem and keep this from ever happening again. You can then ask them if they think the company can solve this problem or not.

When to Approach

This conversation should be approached as soon as possible after the employee has been caught overcharging expenses. You shouldn't wait too long to confront them, because if you do, they could begin covering their tracks before you can get to the bottom of things.

Final Tips

Get all the facts together and then think about how you want to proceed. This will help you maintain control of the situation. Remember, it is not about placing blame; rather, it is about solving the problem.

Don't rush into this conversation angry or accusatory because this conversation can easily get out of control if you do. Remember that the company is bigger than any one person's mistake.

Ask for their side of the story. If possible, try to determine if this was a one-time occurrence or something they do frequently.

5. Falsification of Documents

If you are an employer, you are bound to have a conversation at some point about the falsification of documents. You must know the correct procedure for dealing with this issue.

The law states that it is a criminal offense to produce false documents or information. It is also illegal for an employee to use false documents or information while attempting to gain employment, or when being employed. If the employer reasonably believes that the employee has done so, they may terminate their employment and/or report them to the police.

Falsification can occur in many ways and it often involves the use of false documents or information. Examples include:

- An employee is unable to produce a current, valid passport when asked for it.
- An employee misleads the employer as to their qualifications, experience, or any other information that was contained in their CV.
- False references are given, or documents are forged.

- The employee makes an application for a job at another company while still employed with their current company and presents a letter of resignation which has been forged by them, thereby misrepresenting themselves as being available for work.

Best Approach

It is a good idea to speak with your employee in the presence of another employee so that they don't feel intimidated. However, you shouldn't accuse them of falsifying documents without having any evidence. Instead, approach the subject by introducing it as a general conversation about what you know about the employee and how they have been performing in their role.

When discussing this with your employee, be sure to remain calm and do not use accusatory or threatening language.

If you have any doubts about the validity of any documents, then it is always best to ask your employee for another copy before you decide.

When to Approach

It is a good idea to speak with your employee as soon as you become aware of the situation. If the falsification does not relate to their current employment, then it is better to speak with them at the earliest opportunity so that they are aware of your concerns and why you have decided to take this action.

What toto Say

"I am concerned about some of the documentation that you have produced. The documents are dated from a period which is when you were no longer working for us. I would like to understand why this has happened and to discuss this with you."

Final Tips

When speaking with your employee, it is always important to remain calm and avoid using accusatory language. Make sure that you discuss the matter with your employee face-to-face and that another employee is present. If you have any doubts about the validity of any documents, then it is always best to ask your employee for another copy before you decide.

If your employee is unable to give you an explanation, then terminate their employment immediately. If they continue to falsify their documents without your consent or knowledge, then terminate their employment immediately.

If you believe that an employee has falsified documents, then you must seek legal advice before taking any action.

6. Employee Overpayment or Underpayment

The most common form of employee overpayment or underpayment occurs when an employee is paid for some time while not working. For example, an employee may be on approved leave or suspended without pay. The employer may also make errors in calculating the amount of leave an employee has accrued.

Best Approach

This conversation is still difficult because the employee will likely feel embarrassed or angry that the employer found the mistake. The employer should apologize for any inconvenience, and they should discuss how it has happened and why it must be corrected.

The employer should also explain that all errors will be investigated once they are brought to light.

The error could have occurred because of a variety of reasons. It is important to determine whether there was a problem with the systems used for payroll or whether there was an error made by an individual who inputs the data into those systems.

When to Approach

Anytime an employer realizes that an employee has been overpaid or underpaid.

What to Say

"I am concerned to hear that you have been overpaid or underpaid. This is a mistake that I would like to take the time to discuss with you now so it can be corrected."

"I recognize that this may be a difficult situation for you, but I want to assure you that this is not because I do not trust your work or your integrity. This is simply due to an error in the system, and it needs to be corrected."

Final Tips

Remind the employee that this does not reflect on their job performance, and that the employer recognizes that this is an error. Explain how it happened and how, going forward, the error will be avoided.

Employers should also recognize that this is an awkward conversation to have with employees, but they should be prepared for these situations, so they do not happen again in the future.

7. Bribery

This is a tough conversation for both the employer and the employee. Most employees will feel they have a good reason to do what they've done. However, if the company deems it to be a serious offense, they will want to terminate the employee. This is not an easy conversation for either party.

Both parties need to understand what counts as illegal employee bribery and what doesn't. to avoid misunderstandings, this conversation is needed both before and after an employee does something for which they feel they should be compensated. The employer should also be clear with the employee about the consequences of violating company policy regarding employee bribery.

The employee should understand that if he is found guilty of an offense, it may result in his termination. The employee may also be subject to criminal prosecution for accepting bribes and other illegal payments.

Best Approach

The employer should go into the conversation with an open mind. Listen to the employee's explanation and ask questions. The employee should understand that the employer is serious about the issue and that they will not tolerate it in the future.

If both parties have a clear understanding of what is expected of them, this conversation will likely be successful. If either party feels their concerns were not addressed, there should be another meeting to clarify any misunderstandings or misconceptions on either side.

When to Approach

As soon as possible after an offense has been committed. If the employer waits too long, there is a greater chance of misunderstandings. The longer it takes, the more likely it is that neither party will remember what happened. The employer should keep a record of all conversations with employees, including this one.

What to Say

"I have a serious problem that I think has to be addressed. I don't want to embarrass you, but I have to tell you about it. You accepted a $200 gift card from a vendor that represented an illegal payment to you. I'm concerned that you may not understand what happened and why it was wrong."

Final Tips

You should be honest and show concern for the employee. The employer should also remember that they are in charge and need to address the issue head-on.

The employee should understand that the employer is serious about the issue, and that they will not tolerate it in the future.

8. Identity Fraud

Most recently, identity theft has been a hot topic in the news with the number of individuals who have had personal information stolen and used in fraudulent ways.

The biggest challenge for employers is distinguishing between an innocent mistake and criminal activity. Many times, an employer will want to make a quick decision about the extent of damage caused by identity fraud but needs to consider all options before making such a decision.

Best Approach

An employer should approach the employee in a nonconfrontational manner, and let them know that you need to talk about an issue that has arisen. It is important to let the employee know that there is no accusation or judgment, just a desire for information. If possible, have them sit down with you to discuss the situation.

A good approach is to ask questions regarding their experience and what they think happened. If the employee admits to wrongdoing, listen carefully to what they say, and ask questions for clarification. This will help you determine if they are lying or not.

Always be patient when dealing with an employee who has been accused of identity fraud; even if they are guilty, they deserve respect. Also, remember that some employees may feel overwhelmed by trying to explain and defend themselves against allegations of identity fraud; if this is the case, give them time to collect their thoughts before continuing with your line of questioning.

When to Approach

If you believe that your employee is guilty of identity theft, then you should approach them immediately. You can use the above approach to determine who the victim is and what was done to harm them. It may be necessary to contact law enforcement and have a police report filed if property or money was stolen. It will also be necessary to obtain a copy of the police report for your records.

What to Say

"We need your help in determining why someone has used your personal information to commit fraud against our company and an outside party. We need to know what happened so that we can protect ourselves from any further damage and protect others from being harmed by your actions. If you committed identity fraud, we will do everything possible to help you and the victim recover from this situation; however, we want to make sure that you understand the gravity of what you have done."

9. Qualifications Fraud

The more visible and more senior the position, the more likely it is that one of your employees will have a false or exaggerated qualification. The employee will be in great danger of being taken to task by the tax authorities and/or being sued by disgruntled customers or clients.

Qualification fraud has been going on for a very long time, but it has become an increasing problem as qualifications have grown in importance.

Your suspicions should be aroused if you know that your employee has claimed qualifications in addition to those you know about, if you see evidence of a poor attendance record at college, or if your employee cannot explain how he or she achieved high grades in exams. If there is evidence of outright fraud, then you should report this to the police.

Best Approach

Be aware of the possibility of qualification fraud, and be alert for any evidence that it is happening. Keep your eyes and ears open for the following:

- Evidence of poor attendance records at college, especially toward the end of a course.
- Evidence that your employee has claimed qualifications in addition to those you know about.
- Evidence that some or all your employees have claimed qualifications from an institution where they have never been seen.

In all cases, ask yourself what your next step will be if you suspect qualification fraud. If you think that it is particularly likely in a particular case, make an appointment with your employee, and discuss this with him or her before you make any further moves. If you suspect outright fraud, then contact the police immediately.

If you think that it is likely that there has been no crime committed but that your employee has exaggerated or lied about his or her qualifications, then you should talk to him or her about it. You should make it clear what the consequences will be if he or she continues to do so and what the evidence for this is.

When to Approach

Immediately. Don't wait until your annual appraisal. If you delay until the end of the week or month, then it will be too late to report the fraud to the police. Even if there is no evidence that a crime has been committed, talk to your employee as soon as you have any suspicions, and certainly before you decide he or she will be given a job reference in the future.

What to Say

"Can I talk to you about (job title)? The reason I ask is that (reason). May I come in? Thank you. What I want to say is (state what you have noticed and why it makes you suspicious). Is there any explanation for this? Could we go through your other qualifications together? Is there anything else that I should know about?"

"You'll appreciate that if this goes on, we may be able to provide a reference which can only say that 'Jane Smith did such and such on this date, then left us.' If there were any adverse reports about this then we could not give a reference at all. This would be very serious for you if it happened just before an application was made for a job. I hope that we can sort this out, but if we can't then I'll have to report it to my senior managers."

Final Tips

If you suspect qualification fraud and talk to your employee about it, listen to his or her side of the story, and then let him/her know what will happen if he/she does not change his/her ways. If there is evidence of fraud, then contact the police immediately and report any other suspected cases to your senior managers so that they can decide whether they want their employees to have references in the future.

Individual Appearance

This chapter is about employee appearance and how to handle issues related to specific employee appearance. The idea here is that there are times when the employee's appearance may be hurting his or her performance.

This is not an area in which you should be making a judgment call—this should be a professionally designed policy that applies equally to everyone in the workplace, and it should be applied consistently.

10. Poor Dress and Grooming Standards

Everyone knows that the clothes you wear can have an impact on how you are perceived by others. However, sometimes people ignore this fact and still do not dress properly for work.

Poor dress and grooming standards can be a distraction to the organization. They can also lead to the decline of productivity, decrease employee morale, and cause people to have a negative perception of you.

If employees are not dressing appropriately, they will be seen as disrespectful and unprofessional. This will cause your business to lose out on opportunities from customers as well as employees who might want to work for your organization.

Best Approach

When you talk with an employee about their poor dress and grooming standards, make sure that you are calm. If you come at them aggressively, they will just get defensive.

Also, let them know that they are not living up to the standards of the organization and that your concern is coming from a place of professionalism. The employee needs to understand that if they are seen as disrespectful or unprofessional, then it will hurt them in both their personal and professional lives.

When to Approach

You will want to approach this conversation when you have noticed that the employee has a significant problem with their dress or grooming. You will not want to approach them on the first day of work if they are showing up in poor dressing or grooming standards.

What to Say

"I appreciate you coming to work every day, and I know that it is not always easy. However, I feel that it is necessary to bring up an issue with your dress and grooming standards. I have noticed that you are not wearing appropriate clothing for the environment around you."

"I understand that it can be difficult to make sure that you are dressed appropriately for every situation. However, if you would like to convince others of how professional and serious you are about your career, then you will want to make sure that your appearance is on point at all times."

Final Tips

Make sure that you are tactful when you approach this topic. You do not want to come off as rude or condescending.

Also, make sure that this is a consistent problem. If your employee has been dressing and grooming poorly for a while, then you will want to address it sooner rather than later.

You should also be aware of your employee's concerns and what they might think of the conversation with you. If they have been dressing inappropriately because they are concerned about what their coworkers will think, then you will need to reassure them that there is nothing wrong with having high standards of professionalism at work.

11. Shaving Standards for Men in the Workplace

You have finally found the right employee. They are willing to do anything you ask them to, work any hours you need, and have a great attitude.

Then there is the issue of their appearance. The employee is sporting some serious stubble, which is causing an uproar amongst your customers. You can see where this conversation is going.

Best Approach

The best approach is to talk to the employee in a private setting and to use some humor when you come to the subject. Don't use an accusatory tone, but, rather, be straightforward about your concerns.

If you have any examples of how their appearance is not appealing to your customers, bring those along for good measure. If you can get the employee laughing about the situation, they will be much more inclined to make a change and will have a happier work environment.

When to Approach

The best time to approach your employee is when they are not in the middle of doing something urgent. It also will not go over well if you approach them in front of other employees. If you can get them alone in a small room, you can easily bring up the issue. Remember, lighten the mood by using some humor, and they will be far more receptive to your concerns.

What to Say

A proper conversation should start with some small talk, but the main topic should be discussed right away.

Start by saying "I've noticed you are quite happy with your work here and your attitude is great. However, I have noticed that you have a bit of a beard growing under your chin and a mustache coming in."

Make sure they understand that it isn't about "looking good" or trying to be vain—it is simply about being professional and presenting themselves as being well-groomed and appealing to the customer who has come in for an enjoyable experience at your business. If they ask for any examples from customers who have complained, provide them with a few.

Final Tips

Asking your employee to shave their facial hair may seem like a silly issue, but it is important to understand that it is a representation of your company's culture.

Having a set of guidelines or a clear reason why you make this request will allow you to have a better understanding of what is acceptable. The key is to be consistent. If you apply the rules to every employee and uphold the grooming standards, you will have fewer complaints in the long run.

Remember, the bottom line is that you are the employer, and you can set the guidelines for your company.

12. Women's Hair Length and Style at Work

Up until the early 1980s, it was common for women to work in offices while wearing a short hairstyle. The most popular styles were the pixie cut and the bob. Then, along came "Big Hair" —a woman's long hairstyle popularized by actress Farrah Fawcett in the 70s.

Of course, there is nothing wrong with long hair. However, because it was so popular, many working women opted to grow their hair out longer than they would have otherwise.

To be clear (and for legal purposes), I am not suggesting that any employer should do anything or require any woman to change her hairstyle if she does not want to do so.

However, this does happen. And so, you will need to decide how you want your company to address this issue with its employees when it arises in your workplace.

Best Approach

The best approach is generally to let the employee know where you stand on this issue, and that you will consider all factors in evaluating your employee's performance and conduct in a fair manner.

You may want to also add that your company makes exceptions to its policies for non-work-related appearances (such as dress code), and that there are exceptions to this policy as well.

If you are planning on having a meeting with your employee(s) about their hair style or hair length, it would be wise to include your supervisor or Human Resources representative in the meeting to allow them to hear what your concerns are. Also, if you plan on terminating an employee over this issue, I strongly encourage you to get some legal advice before making any decisions.

When to Approach

Of course, there is nothing wrong with long hair. However, unkempt hair is an issue. It is unprofessional. This is a problem that should be addressed. It is best to approach the employee privately.

The employee may simply not know that her hair length and style is out of place. It is best to offer suggestions on how to correct the situation. It is also important to be specific as to what is objectionable about the hair length and style. Be specific as to what would fix the problem. If the employee does not agree with your opinion, it is best to suggest a compromise, such as wearing a hair net or covering her hair with a bandana.

What to Say

"Our company believes that it is important for all of our employees to maintain proper grooming standards at work for our business to present a positive image both inside and outside of the office."

"Although we expect all of our employees not to distract from their work by allowing their attire or appearance (including hair length) to interfere with their ability or reduce the confidence of others around them, we also understand that an employee may want to make a change, such as growing their hair longer, that we may not approve of."

"If an employee's hair length or style (or lack thereof) is causing a distraction or is interfering with the employee's ability to perform their job, the employee will be given one month to correct the problem. If the problem cannot be corrected within one month, the employee should contact Human Resources to discuss further options."

Final Tips

There may be some medical conditions that require a woman to wear a certain hairstyle. You should make sure that you are aware of any medical conditions that might require an employee to wear a longer hairstyle.

Any time you have a policy or rule in place for your employees, it is important to make exceptions when they are justified. "No" is not always the best answer.

13. Tattoos and Piercings: How Much is too Much?

With the changing times, employees have become more open about their personal choices and preferences.

Some of them choose to express their individuality by getting tattoos and piercings. While these employees may look the part, employers must be cautious about how far they can go when regulating the appearance of their employees.

What is a tattoo?

Tattoos are permanent marks or designs made on the skin with a needle or other sharp instruments (including branding) that inflict pigment under the skin to get an image on the skin. These marks are usually created by injecting ink under the surface of your skin from which it stays there permanently.

What is a piercing?

Piercing is the process of creating an opening in your body that can be used for jewelry or decoration. A piercing does not necessarily have to involve an opening in the skin, but more commonly involves the piercing of body parts (such as ears, nose, lips, tongue, or belly button) where the holes are used to attach jewelry.

Best Approach

You should discuss this issue with your employee openly and honestly. You can set up a meeting with the employee to discuss the issue of tattoos and piercings.

You can tell them that you have concerns about the safety of your employees and their ability to do their jobs because of the number or size of tattoos or piercings that they have.

You should then ask the employee if there is a way for him/her to work within these rules that you have set up without being concerned about his/her safety. If they cannot, you can then decide on whether it is okay for them to continue working for you.

When to Approach

You should approach this issue when you are comfortable doing so. You mustn't create an uncomfortable working environment for your employee because of this issue. When you approach them, it is also important that you do not put any pressure on your employee to agree with your concerns.

What to Say

You can say, "I'm concerned that your tattoos or piercings may look unprofessional while you are at work. I know that having tattoos or piercings is a choice that you have made to express yourself, but I also have to think about what is best for my business and the safety of my employees. What do you think would be a good way for us to work around this issue?"

Final Tips

You should be careful to avoid any bias when you are making your decision about how to approach this issue. You should not single out your employee because of his/her appearance or because they have tattoos or piercings.

You should not make any comments that may be perceived as discriminatory.

If you feel that the issue is becoming too much for you, then you may want to consider talking to a professional who can help you handle this sensitive situation.

14. Attitudes Toward Weight: Is Your Company a "Fit" Place to Work?

As a business owner or manager of a business, you must balance your concern for the health and welfare of your employees. In approaching this delicate issue, it's important to bring in an expert who can talk to your employee about weight loss strategies that work while still accommodating their work schedule and needs.

Best Approach

The best approach is to discuss your concerns over a meal of healthy food. It's also important to be aware of the employee's family situation. Discuss possible reasons for weight gain as well as any possible solutions.

It is important to remember that employees are often set in their ways and they may not want to change their eating habits, exercise habits, or lifestyle. It's important to keep these points in mind when discussing weight with an employee.

When to Approach

It's important to set up a time to have this discussion. If you sense the employee is unhealthy, it's probably time to have the discussion. You should also consider scheduling a meeting in which you can discuss your concerns with the employee and possibly their physician.

What to Say

The opening statement is the most important part of this conversation. It's important to express concern for your employee's health in a way that will not be offensive or insulting. Be careful not to criticize your employee over their weight. Instead, express concern over possible health risks such as diabetes, high blood pressure, or heart problems associated with being overweight and how these could affect them as well as your business if they were unable to work because of these conditions.

It's also important to explain that you are concerned for their health and well-being and you want them to be able to enjoy life without health problems associated with obesity. At this point, it's appropriate to ask if they know the risks of being overweight and if they have any solutions for dealing with it and getting healthy again. If they do not have any solutions, then it's okay for you to ask them about their daily eating habits, exercise habits, and lifestyle changes they are willing to make.

For example, "Ms. Smith, I've noticed that you have gained some weight over the last six months. Is there a reason for this? I'm concerned about your health because I want you to be able to have a long and healthy life. Are you aware of the risks associated with obesity? Do you have any ideas on how to lose weight or maintain a healthy lifestyle? Have you discussed this with your physician?"

Final Tips

Do not criticize or insult your employee over their weight. It's important to let them know that they can trust you and that they are not being judged. It's also important to let them know that there is no shame in discussing weight or being overweight. The important thing is to be healthy and enjoy your life.

When discussing exercise and diet with your employee, remember that they are most likely not accustomed to exercising. You should encourage them to start with small steps and build on them.

It's also important for you to work with the employee to set realistic goals that can be reached over time. You can also ask them to share their progress with you so you can give feedback on their progress and help them achieve their goals.

15. Personal Hygiene in the Workplace

This is as sensitive of a topic as it gets. The best way to approach this is to make sure the employee feels comfortable that you are not just confronting them about this issue, but you are helping them fix it.

Most employees will be mortified when confronted about this topic. That is why it is important to approach the conversation in a way that reassures the employee that you are there to help them and not just reprimand them.

Best Approach

Having a conversation like this can be hard if you have never had to have one before. You need to keep in mind, however, that no matter how sensitive the topic may be, you are there to help them.

The goal is to make the employee feel comfortable in their workplace, and if something is going on with their hygiene, then they need to be aware of it and try to fix it.

When to Approach

There is no specific time that you should approach someone about this topic. You should approach the conversation when it feels right to you. If you don't feel comfortable or if it feels like the employee is in a bad mood, then ask them if they can meet after work to talk about personal hygiene and give them some time to think about it.

What to Say

"Mary, I have noticed you have been going through a lot of deodorants lately. Is everything okay? I don't want you to feel uncomfortable about this…but I have noticed a scent coming from your office. It's nothing bad, but it does smell like deodorant that has been on for a while. I wanted to make sure everything was okay with you and your hygiene at work."

Final Tips

The worst thing you can do is confront someone about something like this and then leave them hanging. You need to be sure that the employee feels comfortable and wants to discuss it with you. If they don't, they may feel like there is no way to get out of this situation and it will lead to more issues in the workplace.

16. The Use of Makeup and Cosmetics in the Workplace

Cosmetic use is becoming very popular in the workplace, and it is not uncommon to see employees who are wearing concealer, lipstick, and eye shadow. With makeup, many people can look more attractive and professional; however, some companies do not allow this practice within the work environment.

Best Approach

The best approach to discuss this topic with an employee is, first, to make sure that there is not a current policy in place that specifically prohibits the use of cosmetics. If there is, then there isn't much you can do.

However, if you have an employee who wears makeup and you want them to tone it down at work, then the next step would be to invite them into a private office meeting.

When to Approach

In most cases, you will need to approach an employee about this issue during the initial meeting or a scheduled annual review. Since this is a sensitive topic, you shouldn't bring it up during a casual conversation.

What to Say

When you approach an employee about their makeup, be sure to express your concern. For example, state something like, "I noticed that you are wearing a lot of eye shadow to work and I am concerned that it is distracting other employees from focusing on their work."

Also, be sure to listen carefully to the response you get from your employee. If they do not seem receptive to what you have to say, then just tell them that you are concerned with their distraction and would like them to tone it down at work.

Final Tips

As long as your company does not have a policy against the use of cosmetics in the workplace, then there isn't much else that will need to be said.

However, if you do have a policy in place and your employee still chooses to wear cosmetics, you may need to send a written notice stating that they are violating company policy and ask them not to wear any makeup while at work.

If they continue to violate this policy after receiving the written notice, then you may need to terminate their employment for insubordination or for violating company policies.

17. Body Odor

This is one of the most difficult topics to discuss with your employees, and even if you have discussed it, you will face the same issue again and again.

The reason for this is that people do not like to talk about the smell of their body, and they are quite oblivious about it. But it is crucial to talk about this with your employees as it may have a huge impact on the overall working environment in your office or factory.

Body odor is not something that we can control. Even if we take a shower daily, our body can start smelling after some time, especially in hot weather. So, what you should do about this?

Best Approach

Talk about it with your employees. Even if you think that this may cause embarrassment, it is better to talk about it in the office. This will help you to make your employees aware of this issue and they will start taking the necessary steps to avoid it. For example, if they know that eating garlic can cause body odor, then they may not eat garlic at work.

During the discussion, you should make your employees understand that body odor may cause discomfort among other people, so it is important to take care of this issue. You can also discuss with them which foods or drinks may cause smell in their bodies.

When to Approach

If you are the manager, then you should approach your employees immediately when you notice that they have started smelling bad. If your employees are not aware of their body odor, then they may not take care of it, as they will not be able to distinguish whether they smell bad or not.

So, if you notice that your employee is looking for excuses to leave his/her desk during working hours, then he/she may have started smelling bad.

What to Say

"I don't know how to tell you this, but I think that you have started smelling bad. If you are eating garlic or onion regularly, then it may be the reason for the body odor. Please change your diet and eat food that does not cause a bad smell in your body."

Final Tips

Body odor is a sensitive issue, and you should not talk about it in public. You should talk about it in the office when you are alone with your employee.

If your employee is the cause of body odor, then he/she should take special care of it and try to avoid smelling bad. But if your employee does not know what causes body odor, then he/she will not be able to take care of this issue. So, you have to let him/her know what causes it and how he/she can avoid such smells in his/her body.

18. The Right to Be Different: How to Handle 'Unusual' Dress Styles

The employee has been working for the company for a while with no concerns. The employee dresses in a way that is unacceptable for the workplace. The dress style may include attire that is exposing, unclean, inappropriate, and/or offensive.

Best Approach

This is a very tricky situation. If you make a discrimination complaint against this employee, they might feel even more targeted, and you don't want to do that. The best approach is to have the conversation with the employee, but not in an official setting. In other words, it should be done in a casual way and without any witnesses.

Ask the employee if they have some time to go for coffee or lunch and discuss something with them. Make sure that you are careful how you describe it because you don't want to give them the wrong idea about what is going to happen. Be sure to emphasize that this is not an official meeting and just two friends going for coffee/lunch (if they are friends). If they know that it's not an official meeting, hopefully, it will reduce their anxiety level a bit.

Once the conversation starts, ask them about their background and where they grew up. Ask them if they ever had problems with their dress style growing up or at work. Give them some time to talk about it because they might need some time to warm up to talking about their personal life.

When to Approach

This type of conversation should be approached as soon as you notice that the employee is having a problem with his/her dress style. If you wait too long the situation could get even worse.

It's very important to have this discussion as soon as possible. You don't want it to be pushed off for a long time because that might cause the situation to get worse; and then when you finally have this discussion with them, they might feel "targeted" or "persecuted" because they have been waiting for quite some time to speak with someone about their dress style problems.

What to Say

"I have noticed a recent change in the way that you dress, and I need to talk with you about it. It's not that I don't like the way that you dress, but there are some problems associated with it. You might not realize it, but your current style of dress is causing problems for me and others in our company."

"There are some things that I would like to talk with you about, but first I need to ask: is this is an acceptable time to talk? If not, then please let me know when would be a good time for us to meet."

"I appreciate your willingness to speak with me about this matter. I understand that it can be a difficult topic for many people, and so I thank you for talking with me."

"Before we begin discussing this subject any further, I want to make sure that we are on the same page in terms of language. Are we both using the same type of language? Do you understand what the words 'dress style' mean?"

"Your current style of dress is causing problems for me and others in our company because it violates our company policies which require employees to wear a uniform or professional attire."

Final Tips

You must be careful about the language that you use. You don't want to use any words that could be considered offensive in terms of cultural differences. It's best to avoid using words such as "Arabic" or "Muslim" if they are not part of their culture.

Tell them that you understand how difficult it is for them to find clothes that fit properly and/or are appropriate for the work environment and that you would like to help them find a better solution.

Policy Violations

In every organization, some rules must be followed. In some instances, those rules are written, and in others, they are not. Whether they are written or not, it is important to know what you can and cannot do as an employee to make the workplace a safer environment for everyone.

Employees who are not familiar with the company policies can be a liability to the organization. Employees who are familiar with the rules will be able to follow them and work within the safety parameters of your organization.

This chapter will provide you with some common policies that can be found in an organization and explain how they affect your job functions.

Policy violations are the most common type of violation that occurs in an organization. They include everything from tardiness to theft.

19. Failure to Adhere to Company Safety Guidelines

This is a difficult conversation to have with your employees as it may make them feel like they have failed in some way. However, you must keep your employees safe and adhere to the guidelines set forth by the company. As a manager or supervisor, you may be held responsible if an employee was injured and the company had failed to enforce safety rules.

Best Approach

Do not try to get into a debate with the employee about this. You need to show your concern for their well-being and be firm in your decision. If you can give a sincere explanation that will help them understand why you feel the rules were broken without pointing fingers or being judgmental, this could help them agree with your decision.

Be prepared for emotion and anger, as they may not agree with you. You need to remain calm and patient. Do not get defensive or angry if they get upset. Remember that you are the boss, and do not try to make excuses for the employee's actions.

When to Approach

This conversation should be had as soon as possible after the incident has occurred. If the employee was injured, you need to act quickly to prevent further injury.

What to Say

"John, I want to talk to you about what happened in the plant the other day. We all must adhere to company safety rules. We will not allow anyone to work in a dangerous environment at this company, and I need your help in keeping things safe."

"I know you understand that we have a zero-tolerance policy for failure to adhere to the safety rules. I know that it was not your intention to break those rules, and I realize that sometimes accidents happen. But I need you to be careful after this, so we don't have another accident."

"As a supervisor, I am responsible for enforcing these rules, but if something were to happen and the employee was punished because of it, it would be my fault. We will not let anything like this happen again. So please make sure you understand these rules and follow them carefully."

Final Tips

Stress that you care about the employee's well-being and want to keep them safe. This is important as it will show that you are not blaming them for the accident but are simply doing your job by enforcing the safety rules.

Do not get defensive or angry if the employee gets upset. The conversation should be a positive one, not a negative one. Make sure you talk calmly, and try to answer any questions they may have without making excuses for their actions.

Always follow up with your employees after having this conversation to make sure they understand why you took the action you did and what actions need to be taken to avoid further violations of company safety rules.

20. Inappropriate Conduct with a Customer

The most important conversations you have with employees are those that lead to improved performance, greater job satisfaction, and stronger relationships. But sometimes your intent to help has the opposite effect. Some performance discussions go poorly, and you end up in a worse situation than we had before.

It's easy to feel like a failure after an unsuccessful experience, but the reality is that it takes courage and practice to have these difficult conversations successfully.

Best Approach

The best approach is to remember that difficult conversations are a two-way street. They're about both parties trying to reach the same goal—to achieve a better outcome.

First, you need to be clear on what your goal is. Often, you may think that you want an employee to improve performance. But if your goal is to achieve success for the organization, then your focus should be on helping the employee achieve success first. The more successful the individual is, the more likely it is that he or she will contribute to organizational success.

After you have defined your purpose, it's important to communicate it directly and honestly with the other person. If you have an open, honest relationship with this person, then you can probably do this in person. But if you feel uncomfortable or unsafe doing so, then you can do it on the phone or in writing (e-mail).

When to Approach

This conversation should be done as soon as possible after you've observed the problem behavior or become aware of it. The longer you wait, the harder it is to have an honest conversation because the employee may think that you're just trying to get him or her in trouble.

The best time for this conversation is when you and the employee are both relaxed and in a good mood. Waiting for a moment when he or she is mellow and receptive will help make this easier to handle.

What to Say

First, you want to establish that the problem is the employee. No matter how it looks to you, this is his or her responsibility. Say something like "I have noticed a pattern of behavior that concerns me. I think it is your responsibility, and I'd like us to talk about it."

Be clear about what you want him or her to do differently. For example, "I want you to address customers in a way that makes them feel comfortable and valued so they will recommend our company to others." Then tell him or her what he or she needs to do differently for that goal to be reached (for example, "I want you to speak slower so the customer can understand what you are saying").

Final Tips

Step back from the situation for a moment and get into neutral territory by talking about your own experience as a manager—something we all have in common.

Be careful not to blame the employee for your feelings—that will create defensiveness and make it harder for him or her to hear what you are saying. You want them to feel safe and respected when they talk with you, so speak calmly and remain nonjudgmental.

If the employee seems upset, then you might want to say that you would like to talk with him or her at another time when he or she is more comfortable. If the employee says that he or she is upset, it's important to listen and to acknowledge what he or she is saying without defending yourself.

If you think the employee might be feeling defensive, then it's better to schedule a meeting after things have settled down, rather than having this conversation in the heat of the moment.

21. Personal Use of Company Property or Equipment

It is not uncommon in the workplace for employees to use office equipment or supplies for their own purposes.

In some cases, this misuse can be a minor and infrequent occurrence. In other cases, it may be a more serious and frequent problem.

Best Approach

The best approach for dealing with an employee who uses company equipment or supplies for personal use is to have a direct but nonconfrontational conversation with your employee about it. Make sure that you are tactful and respectful when discussing the issue with your employee, as he or she may be unaware of your company's policy on these matters.

When to Approach

Regardless of the circumstances, it is always important to address this matter with your employee when the misuse occurs, and when you first become aware of it.

What to Say

"I noticed that you used our copy machine to copy documents for a personal project that you are working on. While we appreciate that you wanted to save money by only using one copy machine, it is against company policy for employees to use office equipment or supplies for their projects."

"I want to make sure that you know that it is our policy for employees to use office equipment or supplies only for company business. Please make sure that this does not happen again."

Final Tips

Overall, this is a common issue that you are likely to face as an employer. It is important to handle it in a nonconfrontational manner and with tact and respect, but it is also important not to let this matter slide.

However, if your employee has been using office supplies for their personal use on a regular or consistent basis, it may be appropriate for you to discuss the matter with your company's Human Resources department or legal counsel before proceeding with the conversation.

22. Attendance Policy Violations

There is no easy way to discuss attendance policy violations with your employees, especially if the policy is new. An employee who has been exempt from attendance policy violations may now be subject to disciplinary action for violating the business's attendance or tardiness policy.

Best Approach

When talking to an employee about attendance policy violations, professionally approach the subject. Be objective and firm, but not confrontational or accusatory. The employee is probably aware that he or she has violated the attendance policy, so you may want to begin by stating the facts about the violation.

You should include how many times the employee was late or absent from work and what disciplinary action will be taken if the situation is not corrected immediately.

You may want to state that if there are recurring incidents of tardiness or absences, your company will have no choice but to terminate his or her employment immediately due to a lack of commitment. You should also state that it is impossible for you to effectively manage your business while having an absentee on your staff.

When to Approach

You should talk to an employee about attendance policy violations as soon as possible after the incident occurs. If the employee is on a probationary period, the company may be able to terminate that person for violating your attendance policy due to lack of commitment, even if the violation is not serious enough to warrant termination.

What to Say

"John, I have never had a problem with your attendance. However, it has been brought to my attention that you have repeatedly arrived late for work and have been absent without prior approval on several occasions. This is not acceptable and may result in disciplinary action if you do not make a more serious effort to be here when scheduled."

"If you fail to improve your attendance habits immediately, your employment with our organization may very well be terminated. I will not tolerate an employee who is habitually late for work or who fails to notify me of any absence as soon as possible after returning from a scheduled medical appointment."

Final Tips

Provide the employee with a copy of your attendance policy. It is good to give the employee a chance to read the policy for themselves.

Be clear and specific with the employee about what is expected of them in terms of attendance.

23. Stealing

Stealing is one of the most difficult topics that you can discuss with employees. It will be even more difficult if the employee is your friend.

When you are not able to control your employees, they will take advantage of your kindness.

Employees who steal things either for their use or for sale will become a huge liability for the organization. It is also important that you make it clear to all employees that stealing will not be tolerated in your organization.

Best Approach

Whenever an employee steals something from your organization, you can address the issue by discussing it with the employee in private. If you have not caught the employee stealing but heard about it from others, you should still talk to the employee and ask him/her if it is true. If he/she has done it, make sure that you talk to him/her about why he/she decided to do that and how it can affect your organization if such activities are not stopped.

When to Approach

As soon as you hear about the stealing activity, it is important to address the issue.

What to Say

"We have a situation here at the company. You know you are not supposed to take anything from the workplace, but I heard that you took some paper from the printer room and gave it to one of your friends. Is this true?"

"We are all friends here, but we cannot take advantage of being friends. If you have done this, could you please tell me why you did so and what do you plan to do next time?"

"I am sorry to hear that you did this—this is not acceptable in our organization."

"If you do not stop doing such things, I will have no other choice but to let you go."

"I know we are close friends but if anyone hears about it, it could be very damaging for our organization."

Final Tips

Do not discuss the stealing incident with other employees before talking to the employee who has done it. It may make others feel uncomfortable, and it may affect their performance as well.

If you have a very good relationship with the employee, and he/she is the one who has done it, try to talk to the employee in a way that will make him/her feel comfortable.

Just like other difficult conversations, make sure that you are calm and composed while addressing the issue. It will help you to deliver your message properly.

24. Loss or Damage of Company Property

Accidents happen, and employees will damage or lose company property at some point in their career. The best way to handle this type of situation is to have open communication with employees and discuss the situation in a calm manner.

Best Approach

Whenever possible, it is best to bring the employee into a conversation with you before they leave their shift. A manager should discuss the situation calmly and ask the employee what happened. It is important to do this out of view or hearing of other employees who may gather around to watch. The next step would be to ask the employee if they feel they were at fault and what they think should be done about the situation.

Reviewing the situation together with an open mind and an air of honesty will help establish trust between manager and employee. The employee must understand that any feeling of being treated unfairly is unfounded, and that there will be no discrimination in any action taken against them.

When to Approach

It is best to have this conversation outside of the work environment, and the best time to do this is when the employee is leaving work to go home. If an employee has damaged or lost company property, it is important to discuss this issue as soon as possible.

What to Say

"I noticed that you were involved in an incident on the job that damaged company property. I am concerned about this situation and would like to talk with you about it."

"I want to make sure that I understand what happened. Could you please explain to me what happened?"

"What do you feel should be done about this situation?"

"I would like to help you with this situation. What can we do together so we can both be satisfied with the outcome?"

Final Tips

Make sure you are looking for solutions to the problem and not just how to point fingers at other people. The key to a successful resolution is to be honest, open, and show compassion for the employee that caused the problem. If you lose your temper, you can expect to have a hard time working with this employee in the future.

25. Failure to Adhere to Company Guidelines on Workplace Security

Security is a touchy subject for employees, especially when it comes to security policy violations. The sensitive nature of these types of violations often leads to difficult conversations about the behavior.

Employee failure to adhere to workplace security is a frequent problem with both IT and non-IT employees. This failure is often motivated by personal interests and rarely involves malicious intent.

Best Approach

When speaking with an employee who has failed to adhere to a workplace security policy, it is important to first understand why the behavior occurred.

For example, is the employee aware of the policy and simply neglectful? Is the employee trying to get access to protected information for personal reasons? Or is this a demonstration of malicious intent? Once you have established this information, you can proceed with the conversation in the most appropriate manner.

For these conversations to be helpful and successful, you must handle them in a way that does not put yourself or your organization at legal risk. This means that you must ensure that your actions are within your legal rights as either an IT or non-IT manager.

When to Approach

Inquire into the violation after it has occurred. It is recommended that you wait until the incident is resolved before approaching an employee about a failure to adhere to workplace security.

Approach only after other managerial efforts have failed. If other managerial efforts have been unsuccessful, then it may be time to speak with the employee about the violation using a professional and non-accusatory manner.

What to Say

"I noticed that you violated our workplace security policy when you downloaded these files. This is a violation of company policy, and we must constructively discuss this issue."

"I noticed that you violated our workplace security policy when you downloaded these files. This behavior is unacceptable, and we must discuss this situation immediately."

Final Tips

It is important to be clear with an employee about what they did wrong and why it was wrong. It is also important to be aware that the employee may have other issues that need to be addressed, such as a psychological problem or a personal issue that needs to be resolved.

Ultimately, you must handle these conversations with employees about the failure to adhere to workplace security policies and procedures in a way that protects your organization from further risk. By doing so, you will be able to mitigate the negative effects of this behavior and make sure that it does not occur again in the future.

26. Insubordination

It is important to first define "insubordination," because you will find that the definition of the word itself will be very useful in explaining to your employee why you need to have a difficult conversation with them.

Insubordination is a "willful defiance of authority." There are times when an employee will blatantly ignore your instructions or orders or when they attempt to undermine your position of authority. The best way to deal with this is to confront the issue head-on and early in the process. This can easily be done through a difficult conversation with the employee about insubordination.

Best Approach

The best way to approach this type of difficult conversation with an employee is to have it face-to-face; not over email and not over the phone.

You want it to be as direct as possible so that both parties are not left wondering what was said, or left wondering if they did something wrong and that is why they are being talked to about it.

Confronting an issue directly always yields better results than confronting it indirectly through emails or phone calls. It also allows you as the manager to look at the employees face-to-face and see if they understand what they have done wrong.

When to Approach

There are times when an employee will be insubordinate, and you should approach them about it immediately. This is the case when an employee has been told not to do something by you, and they have chosen to ignore that instruction. This is where the word "willful" comes into play because this means that they have chosen to ignore your instructions on purpose.

What to Say

"I need you to stop what you are doing and sit down with me for a minute."

You need to let the employee know that you want them to come out of their work environment and meet with you. This is so that it will be a direct conversation between the two of you and not an indirect one through an email or phone call.

"I have noticed that you have been [insert behavior]."

This is where you need to let the employee know what they have been doing wrong. This must be a direct statement.

Saying something like, "I noticed that sometimes I hear you talking while someone else is talking," or "I noticed that from time to time I can hear your voice raised in anger," does not provide the employee with specifics on what they did wrong.

On the other hand, saying something like, "I noticed that last week when I asked people to help me get these reports together by Friday, at one point I heard your voice in the office saying, 'we will never get these done by Friday,'" provides specifics, showing the employee exactly what they did wrong.

Final Tips

You should always have difficult conversations with employees about insubordination in a private office setting, not in the hallway or cafeteria. Taking the conversation to a public place can only serve to embarrass the employee, and make them feel as if they are being attacked, or that they are being put on trial for their actions.

27. Substance Abuse

Sometimes an employee will display signs of substance abuse. This can be seen through behavior or unexpected action.

This is something that must be addressed quickly before damages occur within the whole company, such as a drop in production or an increase in expenses.

Best Approach

The best approach to take regarding substance abuse within the workplace is to confront the employee with evidence of inappropriate behavior. This can be done during a difficult conversation with the employee.

However, it is important to make sure you are accurate when confronting your employee about their actions. It is not a good idea to confront an employee based on assumptions. You must be sure that there is enough evidence before confronting your employee about their actions.

When to Approach

An employee must be confronted immediately after they have engaged in any inappropriate behavior. It is not a good idea to wait until the next day or even after lunch to approach your employee about their behavior. It is best to do it right away so that the employee understands that you are serious about addressing their inappropriate behavior.

What to Say

"I've noticed some concerning behavior lately. You seem to be making more errors than usual, and you seem to be getting along less with your coworkers. We need to talk about this."

Final Tips

If your employee tries to deny the inappropriate behavior, you must produce examples of that behavior and explain why that is concerning. If you are unable to produce evidence of wrong-doing, then it may not be a good idea to confront your employee about it.

If you notice any signs of substance abuse within your office, do not hesitate to have a difficult conversation with the employee regarding the issue. You must confront them immediately after noticing the inappropriate behavior so that they understand that you are serious about addressing their actions.

Workplace Attitude

28. Dealing with a Colleague Who Gossips

This is a difficult conversation to have with an employee because of the delicate nature of the topic. Employees gossip about each other and their bosses all the time. A boss who hears about it can either ignore it or confront it head-on.

Ignoring it may make the employee think that what was said is true, which might cause problems with other employees. Confronting it head-on may expose a potential issue that you do not want to be made public knowledge, so, now, decide what to say and how to say it.

Best Approach

First, you need to decide how much you want to get involved in this situation. As a boss, you have the right to investigate if someone is spreading rumors about another employee or you; but as a boss, you also need to be careful not to get too involved in these types of problems.

As a rule of thumb, if what is being said will not harm your company, ignore it. If it might harm your employees or your company in any way, confront the issue head-on.

Remember that the employee who is doing the gossiping may not even realize that what they are saying can hurt anyone else. If they are confronted about it and see the consequences of their actions, they will stop gossiping for good.

When to Approach

The best time to approach this conversation is when office rumors have been circulating for a while. If you wait until everyone knows about what is being said, you will not be able to hide the fact that you are talking to the employee about it. If you wait until it becomes clear that the rumor is true, then you can ask all involved parties to keep what they know private and avoid the problem altogether.

What to Say

"I have heard that you are spreading some office rumors. I would like to talk to you about it."

"I want to let you know that I am not going to tolerate gossiping in my office. Gossiping is harmful and can cause problems between employees or between employees and myself. I expect the people in my office to work together so that we can be the best that we can be. When you gossip about your coworkers, you are taking away their ability to be their best. We need to work together as a team and not against each other. I don't want to have to punish anyone over this, but I will if necessary."

Final Tips

Never confront the employee in public. It is best to have a private conversation about the problem. You want to give the employee a chance to explain their side of things, and you want to be able to ask them questions about what they said without everyone in the office knowing that you are questioning them.

If this conversation does not get his or her point across, then it will be necessary to take more severe actions, such as suspension or termination. Once an employee starts gossiping, he or she needs to understand that their job may be at stake if they do not stop it.

29. Handling an Employee Who Won't Take Work Seriously

Though it's a common occurrence, many business owners of small businesses don't know how to deal with employees who won't take their jobs seriously. There are several reasons why an employee may not take work seriously.

Best Approach

If you notice an employee who is not serious about his/her work, there are a few steps you can take to rectify the situation.

First, you should try to get the employee to buy into the seriousness of the situation. This can be a difficult task, so you must be patient and persistent. In some cases, you will need to change your approach when telling an employee that he or she needs to take work seriously.

Be sure that you speak with the employee face-to-face so that he or she can see your commitment as well as communicate with you. You may also want to try sending an email or letter detailing expectations and explaining how you expect them to handle any issues regarding this matter.

When to Approach

You should approach employees about taking their jobs seriously as soon as you notice that they are not doing so. You may also want to review your employment contract with them and explain how serious their work is to the company. While it's important to be patient and persistent in these situations, you should also be aware of the time it takes for results.

What to Say

"I'm concerned about your recent performance. I've noticed that you've been taking some shortcuts and not following company policies. I want to make sure that this is a one-time mistake, and that you will try to take your work more seriously in the future."

"I don't think you're taking your work seriously. Your performance has been slipping lately, and I'm concerned that this is a trend we will see continue. I expect you to take your work more seriously to meet the expectations of our company, or else we may have to let you go."

Final Tips

Be patient and persistent. You need to be willing to wait at least a month before expecting a resolution to the situation. However, you should be aware of how long it's taking and should review the situation each week as well.

Enlist the help of employees who are serious about their work. In some cases, these employees may be able to address the situation with the employee who isn't taking work seriously. In other cases, they may be able to witness what is occurring to support your decision that this matter must be handled.

30. Employee Who's Always Late for Meetings

It's never easy to confront an employee about their tardiness, but there are some things you can do to make the process easier.

Best Approach

At the next meeting with your employees, explain to them that you want to nip tardiness in the bud. Tell them that you know they are all busy and have a lot on their plates, but that you don't want meetings to ever start late because of someone's distraction.

Then, ask for examples of people who are always late or who have been distracted during meetings. Make sure you get specific examples so you can talk about the problem clearly and directly with the employee who is causing it (or is distracting others).

When to Approach

This is a discussion that you need to have before the problem becomes a big issue. If you wait too long, you run the risk of other employees seeing this employee as just another slacker.

What to Say

"I see that we have had some issues with meetings starting late recently. I want to know if there is one person who has been more responsible for this than others. We want to get out of the habit of meetings starting late because it takes away from the productivity of everyone in this group."

"I'd like to hear some examples of people who have been late or distracted during meetings so we can discuss it with that person and work on getting these issues resolved."

Final Tips

Be sure to discuss with the employee directly, and make sure you're specific about how they are not being professional. Use examples of their bad behavior to illustrate your point.

Be sure that everyone in the meeting is on board with having this discussion and will not be offended if you address them directly about their part in the problem. If they feel that their contribution is minor, or that it's not fair to single them out, they may feel resentful, and it could slow down progress on fixing the issue.

31. Employee Who Doesn't Produce Quality Work

An employee of yours performs work that is below your standards. You must discuss something with your employee but don't know how.

Best Approach

Schedule a meeting sometime in the future and communicate that the meeting will be focused on this specific issue so the employee can prepare for it accordingly and bring any information that might help explain his/her position (if there is one), as well as learn more about your position.

Understand you may be talking to an employee who is under a lot of pressure. If you are, make sure that you give them some time before you talk to them again. This will let them know that you care about them and their well-being, not just the work they do for you.

When talking with your employee, make sure that your tone is calm, clear, direct, honest, and sincere. Explain what your expectations are for his or her performance and explain what his or her performance has been like so far.

When to Approach

You should approach this conversation as soon as possible. If this is a serious issue, you want to talk to the employee about it before it gets too big.

What to Say

"I have noticed that (state what specifically has been noticed). This is not what I expect from you (or if it's not what someone else expects, explain who else it is). I am concerned about this because... (state why you are concerned)."

"I want to ask some questions. Please don't take this personally; the questions are only to try and understand how you feel about what's going on. What do you think is happening?"

Final Tips

Remember not to make this conversation about yourself. If you do, the employee will be more interested in defending himself/herself than thinking about how he/she can improve.

Also, remember that this is about the employee's performance and not his or her personality. You want your employees to be happy at work, but you don't want them to be happy if their work is not up to your standards.

32. Lack of Professionalism in the Workplace

The conversation should be handled in a business-like manner without emotion. The employee should be made aware that his or her actions are unacceptable and future occurrences will result in disciplinary action.

It is important to listen to the employee's side of the story and to show empathy for his or her feelings. The employee should also be made aware that the behavior is not acceptable in the workplace and that it will not be tolerated again.

Best Approach

The employee should be advised that the behavior is unacceptable and that if it occurs again, disciplinary action will be taken. The supervisor should ask the employee if he or she has any questions and end the conversation. The supervisor should take notes regarding the conversation and be prepared to document any future occurrences of this type.

When to Approach

The supervisor should discuss the issue when the employee has time to devote to the conversation and when he or she is in a calm state of mind.

What to Say

"I have noticed that you have been dressing sloppily at work. Your clothing, hair, and makeup are not appropriate for the office. I am asking you to dress more professionally at work, because your appearance is interfering with the success of our department. If this behavior continues, I will have to take disciplinary action."

Final Tips

The supervisor should remain calm, listen to the employee's side of the story, and show empathy for his or her feelings. Supervisors should also be aware that it is important to document all occurrences when an employee does not dress professionally at work.

33. Employee Who's Unable to Work Well with Others

When work environments have unhappy employees, it can affect the output and productivity of the entire company. If an employee is not working well with others, it could affect other employees, it could affect customers, and it can make the job more stressful for everyone in the office.

Employees are unhappy because of how they are treated at work or because of how they feel about their job. It is important for management to treat all employees fairly and provide them with a good working environment.

Best Approach

The best approach to this difficult conversation is to be direct and honest with the employee. Explain to the employee that he or she is not working well with others and explain why. Give an example of how the employee may be causing conflicts with coworkers or how it is affecting the productivity of the business.

Tell the employee that you do not want him or her to leave, and that you do not want him or her to qui,t but explain that his or her behavior needs to change for the sake of the business.

When to Approach

It is best to approach this topic as soon as possible. The employee needs to know that his or her behavior is affecting the business, and it needs to be corrected. If it is a small problem, then it can be corrected easily. However, if it is a larger problem, then the longer you wait, the worse it will get.

What to Say

"Our company will not succeed if the employees do not work well with each other. Our customers want to be treated professionally, and they do not want to deal with unhappy employees. They want the business to be successful. I am concerned about your behavior with some of the other employees in this office. We need you to work well with everyone else so that we can continue to grow as a company and make our customers happy."

"It would help me if you can explain what is going on in your mind that causes you to act this way or feel this way."

"I would like for us to work together and resolve this issue so that we can continue moving forward."

Final Tips

If the employee does not change his behavior, then it is time to talk to the employee's boss. This requires a difficult conversation about how the employee is not performing well at work and that his or her behavior with coworkers needs to be changed. It is best if you approach this topic directly with the employee and try to resolve it before you need to involve his or her boss.

Some employees will never change their behavior no matter how much they are reprimanded or encouraged. If that is the case, then it may be best for them to leave the company. It is never easy to let someone go, but sometimes it may be necessary.

34. Employee Who Lacks Motivation

It is very difficult to talk to an employee who is lacking in motivation. They are not happy with their job or with the company and they are not going to do anything about it. So, you must figure out a way to get them motivated again.

Best Approach

Start by telling them how much you appreciate them. Tell them you know it's not their fault and that you know they can do a lot better job themselves. Tell them that the time is right to start looking for something better. Ask if they have any ideas or places they could go that would be a better fit for them.

You want to ask your employee what is wrong, what else would they like to do, and whether or not they are happy in the current position.

When to Approach

This is something you need to approach them about as soon as possible. It is important to talk to them right away because they need something better, and they do not want to wait around for it. At the very least, you should have a brief conversation with them about whether or not they are happy in their position and what kind of things might motivate them even more.

What to Say

"I know this is hard for you, but I am concerned about your lack of motivation. You are a great employee, and I would hate to see you just go downhill. Do you have any ideas as to why this is happening?"

"I know that things haven't been going well recently, but I'd like to see you continue to be happy here at the office. Is there anything that could change that would make you want to stay? What do you like about working here?"

"It was brought to my attention that your motivation has taken a turn for the worse recently. Would it be alright if we talked about it for a few minutes?"

Final Tips

Even after you have talked to your employee about their lack of motivation, they may not be motivated right away. You will need to give them time to think about things and figure out the best way for them to proceed. Give them a few days or a week at the very least.

If they do not seem motivated, it is important to keep on top of the situation. Don't just let it go, because if you do, they may start coming into work later and leaving earlier than usual. This is something that can have a major negative impact on your whole company, so you want to be sure to get it fixed right away if it does happen.

If you do not feel like you can motivate your employee properly, you might want to consider getting professional help from an outside source such as a supervisor or Human Resources department member. They may be able to help you find ways to motivate your employee more easily than trying on your own, which could save a lot of time and frustration in the end.

35. Employee Who Constantly Asks for Extra Time Off

Some employees feel that it is okay to take time off whenever they want it, but others know this is not right. The company needs someone who will be there for their job all the time, not just when they feel like being there.

When an employee is constantly asking for extra days off, this could lead to more work for other employees and causing further trouble. If this is a common occurrence, then it is very important to have a conversation with the employee, and let them know they cannot have time off whenever they want it.

Best Approach

You should approach the employee in question and tell them that you have noticed they have been taking a lot of time off lately. You could mention that this is causing trouble for other employees in the company. You should let the employee know that you are willing to work with them and figure out a way to compromise. For example, you could offer to let the employee come in later or leave early on days they feel sick. You should tell the employee that you do not want them to feel uncomfortable or ashamed for needing time off.

However, if the employee is constantly asking for extra time off for vacation, this could be problematic. This is because the employee could be taking time off for vacation on days that are more important.

It is crucial to approach the employee and talk to them about the company's vacation policy. Explain to the employee that the policy states they cannot take off more than x days at a time, or they will not be able to take off at all.

When to Approach

The person in question should be approached right away. If you let this continue to happen, it will lead to problems for the company and the employee could get fired.

What to Say

"I have noticed you have been taking a lot of time off lately. You know that we are a small company and we do not have much time to fill in for you when you are not here. This means we must work harder and take more time out of our own schedules to complete your work. I am wondering if you are having some medical issues which could be causing you to feel sick more often. If you are, I completely understand and would like to help you figure out a way to make it work. For example, we could send you home early on the days you feel sick, or I could work with you on a schedule that would allow you to come in later for days you feel sick."

"I have noticed that you have been taking a lot of vacation time off, and this is causing problems for the company. In the company's vacation policy, it states that employees cannot take off more than x days at once or they will not be able to take off at all."

Final Tips

Be careful, and do not get too aggressive on this one. You do not want to come off as a bully who is trying to control your employee's life. The goal here is simply to get them to open up and talk about what is really going on. It is also a good idea to make sure your employee knows that you are open to providing some flexibility if they are facing some hard times.

36. Long Lunches and Breaks

It is a problem if employees in your office are taking a lot of long lunches or breaks. You must regularly discuss the issue with them and tell them that you are not happy about it. It is important to begin the conversation by looking at the overall picture first to see what is causing so many long lunches.

Best Approach

Communicate to the employee that you are not happy about the number of breaks and lunches that they are taking. Tell them how it is affecting the work overall. Ask them why they are taking so many breaks and lunches.

If they ask you why you are not happy about it, tell them that it is affecting the overall work of the company. Explain to them how it is affecting the other employees and how it is creating problems for them.

You will have to tell them how important their work is and how you need them to come in on time every day and finish their work. Tell them that if they still do not care about their job, then you will have to take action against them. Tell them what that action will be if they do not shape up.

When to Approach

This is something that you need to be discussing with your employee regularly. This is not a one-time thing that can happen and then is forgotten about. You need to bring this up every so often until they stop taking long lunches and breaks.

If you have tried talking to them about it and they haven't stopped then you need to come up with a new approach. You may even want to consider letting them go if they are not going to change their ways.

What to Say

"I am not happy with the amount of time that you are taking off in the office. I know that it is not affecting everyone, but it is still a problem. I need you to come to work on time and finish your work each day."

"I know that you think this is not affecting your work, but it is. The work of the company is important, and you need to get it done."

"You need to come to work on time and finish your work. You are setting a bad example for the other employees if you keep taking so many breaks."

"If you are not going to change your ways then I am going to have to let you go. I don't want that to happen, but I can't let you take advantage of the company like this."

Final Tips

Make sure you look at the overall picture before you approach your employee about their long lunches and breaks. You want to make sure that they aren't taking long lunches and breaks because of something else. For example, they may be getting tired in the afternoon because they are having problems with their schedule. If this is the case, then you need to talk to them about it. They may be working too many hours in a day.

37. Employee Who Doesn't Listen

People who don't listen are a problem for leaders. The most successful leaders in the world have created a workplace where people listen to them. Employees who don't listen hurt their effectiveness and are a problem for leaders.

Best Approach

The best approach to discussing the difficult subject of someone not listening to you is to do it in private. This helps prevent the situation from escalating.

At the beginning of the conversation, you should ask them if they have any idea why you might be upset with them. If they don't know, you will begin by telling them what it is they are doing that upsets you. This will help prevent any false assumptions on their part and lets them know what specifically they need to change.

When to Approach

The best time to approach the subject is before it gets out of hand, and they become too comfortable in their current behavior.

What to Say

"John, I have noticed that there is a pattern in your performance where you don't listen to me. I don't know if this stems from any personal issues you are having or if it is because I am a woman leader. But either way, it is hurting my ability to coach you and leads me to believe that you don't respect me or the work that I am doing here."

"I have noticed this in meetings, one-on-one conversations, and when reviewing your work. It has come to the point where I feel like our work relationship is suffering, and it also hurts our ability as a team to accomplish our goals together."

"I am not sure if there are some underlying problems here or if this is just a personal issue you have with me, but either way, it needs to stop. If it continues, I may be forced into taking measures such as giving you a warning or even terminating your employment."

Final Tips

Be careful of the words you use when having this discussion. If you are aggressive or too harsh, it will hurt your relationship with the employee and cause them to not listen to you in the future.

Also try to avoid using phrases that make the employee feel wrong, like "you don't respect me" or "you don't respect my work." Instead, focus on what they are doing that makes you feel this way, and how it is hurting their performance and your leadership ability.

38. Pathological Liars

It is difficult to have a conversation with an employee that cannot stop lying because they are pathological liars. It is essential to have this difficult conversation with the employee. They give the impression that they are lying to gain trust, or that they lie when they get nervous, or that they lie because they are stupid.

They may claim to be telling the truth because it is true in their mind. They may claim that the liar was told something different and therefore lied. They may claim to not know what was going on. The employee does not understand why he or she needs to tell you the truth.

The talk about pathological liars is an essential difficult discussion because it will give a framework for having further difficult conversations about lying for whatever reason, and it will give a framework for having further difficult conversations about how you expect your employees to tell the truth during all discussions at work and outside of work.

Best Approach

The best approach to this difficult conversation is to discuss with the liar that you have the right to know what is true and what is false. You will, therefore, require that the employee tell you the truth.

You are having this difficult talk because you cannot trust them when they give information. The employee must agree to tell you the truth and they must understand why it is important to tell the truth. The make or break in this talk with the liar is for them to admit that they lied by denying the truth and then agreeing that they must tell you the truth.

When to Approach

The difficult conversation about pathological liars should be held before they tell another lie. If you wait too long, then the employee may believe that you do not care and that there is no purpose in telling the truth. The employee may also believe that it is useless to tell the truth, because it will not change anything.

What to Say

"I am having a difficult conversation with you because I cannot trust you. I need to know what is true and what is a lie."

"I want you to understand that lying destroys trust, and that I will no longer be able to trust you if you continue to lie."

"I am not going to tell you how many times you have lied, but I do expect that in the future you will tell me the truth. You have lied so many times in the past that I cannot take anything that is said at face value without proof. You must understand that if we are going to work together, then we need to deal with this issue of lying."

"I expect you not only to tell me the truth when we talk about issues at work but also when we talk about issues outside of work. You must realize that if there are problems at home or school and they are important enough for us to discuss, then I must know if what was said was true or not. Do you agree?"

Final Tips

A difficult conversation about pathological liars is the beginning of a long process to rebuild trust. The reason for the difficult conversation is so that you can have further discussions with the liar.

You must make it clear that you care about them and only want them to be honest. It is not the intention of this difficult discussion to hurt their feelings, and it is not your intention to make them feel guilty or stupid for lying.

It is appropriate to give them examples where they lied so that they understand why you cannot trust them. It is also important for you to understand why they lied and what they thought would happen if they told the truth.

The liar does not expect you to be angry at him or her but may be surprised at the fact that there are consequences for lying.

39. An Employee Who Won't Accept Your Authority

If your employee does not accept your authority, you might have to take some disciplinary steps. But before you do this, you should try to resolve the issue calmly. The problem is that it can be hard for a manager to keep his or her calm while discussing a problem with an employee. It's important to remember that if you lose control of your emotions, you are likely to say something that will make the situation worse.

Best Approach

You should approach this conversation with an open mind. If you are too emotional, you might just try to steamroll the employee, which will only make her or him even more resistant to your authority.

When to Approach

Ideally, you should approach this conversation when you are not close to a deadline. The employee might be feeling pressured under a tight deadline, and this could cause him or her to lose his or her temper.

It's also best if you can approach this conversation when the employee is at work. This way, he or she will not feel uncomfortable about being there. The problem may be causing the employee to lose interest in work altogether, and he or she might only agree to talk about it if you do so at work.

What to Say

"I have noticed that you are not performing at your best level. I realize that you are not happy with the way I am currently managing this department. I would like us to discuss this issue so we can figure out how to resolve it together."

"I know you might be afraid of losing your job, but I want to make sure that we can work together to resolve any problems in your performance."

"If something is bothering you about the way the department is being managed, I want you to feel free to talk about it with me."

"I realize that there may be some differences between us, but we both want the same thing—for this department to function as well as possible. Let's try to figure out how we can resolve our differences and work together."

Final Tips

If you are managing a team, it's important to remember that employees sometimes feel intimidated by managers. You should make sure that they know you are willing to listen to their concerns and learn from them.

You should also try to act on any recommendations they might have for improving your management skills. This can show the employee that you care about his or her opinions. It will also help build trust between you and your team members.

40. Unexcused Absence that Disrupts the Team's Workload

This is a difficult conversation to have with employees, as there are many different circumstances that can lead to unexcused absences. If an employee is consistently absent, you may want to meet with the employee to discuss your concerns.

It involves discussing which employee does not contribute to the overall teamwork and is causing problems. Also, it is important to be rational, present facts that are based on true data, build a case that justifies disciplinary action, and follow through accordingly.

Best Approach

The best approach is to identify the problem employee in advance. It may be necessary to prepare a list of all employees and their positive and negative contributions. Once the list is completed, it may be necessary to eliminate unproductive employees that do not contribute.

When using this approach, it is possible to positively affirm good performance from other employees without making the problem employee feel threatened. A manager can also discuss the importance of efficient work time management with others on the team. When done right, this will avoid any resentment among other team members who are doing their jobs well.

When to Approach

The best time to have this conversation is when it can be done in private, when both parties are calm and not in the middle of a heated discussion. It is also important to tell the employee you will be talking about the unexcused absence and not the employee's performance. It should be done when the employee is on time or early to work. Doing so will prevent the unexcused absence from becoming an issue. The manager should ask the employee why he/she missed work and why he/she did not notify management.

What to Say

"I noticed that you didn't come in on Tuesday. Was there a reason you missed work?"

"I saw that you were late to work again on Thursday. It's important to be on time for the entire team."

"I noticed that you were absent for two days in a row without permission, and I'll need an explanation for your absence."

"I noticed that you were late three times last month. Please set up a time to meet with me to discuss this further."

Final Tips

This conversation is important because it gives the manager a chance to discuss the problem with the employee and to identify if there is a reason for his/her actions.

If the manager can provide facts, then he/she will be able to justify disciplinary action. However, it's important not to make any threats or conclusions about what will happen if this behavior continues in the future. For example, "This is your last warning."

41. Absenteeism and Employee Inaction

When employees fail to do their jobs, they become a liability to the business. A manager must be able to recognize when an employee is not doing their job properly and then address the issue.

When an employee is chronically absent, it can be a difficult conversation for a manager. An employer must recognize when attendance becomes a problem and then have a difficult conversation with the employee about improving attendance.

Best Approach

The best approach to having a difficult conversation about attendance problems is to speak in a private setting. It is important to speak with the employee in a private setting so that the employee does not feel uncomfortable or intimidated. This will allow an employer to speak directly and honestly with the employee about their attendance problems.

The employer should be honest, but also should focus on being positive and offering help. The manager should not have any preconceived notions about how the employee will react. An employer needs to act professionally and treat all employees fairly and equally.

It is also important for a manager to be prepared for what might happen once they have had a difficult conversation about attendance problems. An employer may be surprised by how their employees react to being confronted regarding their attendance issues.

When to Approach

An employer should approach an employee about attendance issues when there are consistent problems with absenteeism. One of the more effective ways to address the problem is to speak with the employee one-on-one. Employers need to be prepared when approaching employees regarding attendance issues.

What to Say

"I have noticed that you have been absent from work more than normal. This is a problem, and I would like to speak with you about it."

"I am concerned about your attendance this month. You are not at work as much as you should be. I would like to have a conversation about this problem so that we can discuss possible solutions."

Final Tips

Employers need to treat all employees equally. Employers must not allow themselves to become personal about an employee's attendance issues. Employers need to address an employee on a professional level when addressing an employee's attendance problems.

42. Egregious Personal Behavior (Drunk Driving, Drug Use, Sexual Activity at Work)

Most employees who commit egregious acts do not do so with malicious intent. In most cases, they are the same types of employees who work hard, are generally well-liked, and display good judgment in most areas. But when a manager or supervisor is faced with an employee who has been caught engaging in some type of egregious personal behavior, he or she needs to have a clear understanding of what to do about it.

Because of its potentially destructive nature, though, no matter what action is taken by management regarding this type of behavior, it will not be well received by everyone all of the time. Some people are going to be upset regardless of what action is taken, and that's just a fact that needs to be accepted by management.

Best Approach

There are two distinct parts to this discussion: the employee's behavior and the ramifications of that behavior on everyone else at the workplace. The first part of this discussion needs to be handled with tact and compassion.

At this point, the manager or supervisor needs to express his or her concerns about what happened. The employee must understand that the manager or supervisor is not just concerned about what he or she did, but is also concerned about how it will impact others.

Following this initial conversation, it is important for management to communicate what action will be taken in response to this type of behavior.

Depending on the offense, there are all sorts of possible outcomes. Some offenses can be wiped clean by a sincere apology and a promise never to repeat them. Others may require some form of disciplinary action, perhaps suspension without pay for a certain amount of time or even termination.

When to Approach

While this is a difficult conversation to have, it's best to approach it as soon as possible after the fact. The sooner the employee knows how management feels about what he or she has done, the sooner he or she can come back from this type of behavior and get back on track. The longer management waits to confront an employee, the harder it will be for that employee to forget about what happened and get on with his or her job.

What to Say

"I'm concerned about what happened, but I'm also concerned about how it will impact the rest of the team."

"I know you have a lot of other responsibilities to take care of, but I need you to help me monitor this situation. If you see any other employees doing these things, let me know as soon as possible."

"I hope that we can all move past this and get back on track. I realize that you may have some lingering concerns about how I handled this or what action I took in response, but I want to assure you that my decision was made in good faith and with everyone's best interests in mind."

"I do trust that you will do your best to make sure this doesn't happen again."

Final Tips

Employees who have engaged in egregious personal behavior will sometimes try and make excuses for their actions. It's important for management to understand that they are not responsible for making excuses or providing any type of justification. The only thing they need to do is to communicate clearly what action they expect from the employee in the future and how they expect others to help in monitoring the situation.

Complimenting them on their hard work and effort can help them see that you care about them personally as well as professionally, which can go a long way toward helping them move past any residual tensions that may remain after having this difficult conversation.

Termination

In this chapter, we are going to discuss the termination of an employee. This is probably the most difficult situation a manager must handle. It can be very stressful for the manager, especially when he/she knows that they might be the cause of someone losing their job.

There are two ways that employees can be terminated:

1.   Voluntary—The employee chooses to leave of their own free will.
2.   Involuntary—The employee is fired.

The termination process should always begin with a conversation with the employee. This conversation is usually done informally, just between the manager and the employee.

The manager should always start by asking the employee what their reason for leaving is. This lets the employee feel like they are being heard and that they have control of their situation.

At this time it is important to prepare for the next step of the termination process. Make sure that you take notes on what the employee says because this will later help you determine if you are going to use a formal or informal exit interview. If you are going to conduct a formal exit interview (which we will discuss in a moment) then you need to make sure that you have all your notes prepared beforehand so that they will be available when needed.

Here are examples of some difficult conversations that may need to be addressed.

43. How to Handle an Employee Who Just Won't Leave

One of the hardest things for a manager to deal with is an employee or staff member who just refuses to leave. When they don't want to go, there is not much you can do short of getting the law involved.

Best Approach

The best approach when an employee will not leave after closing time is to calmly tell them that they are expected to be on time for work and to leave when their shift is over. They may need a few reminders of this before they realize what you expect from them.

It can be threatening when they are just standing there watching you and staring at you, but it is important not to take their behavior personally or to get into a confrontation with them.

Be prepared that the employee may become angry or even threaten you before he/she leaves, but hopefully, most employees will not do this and should just leave on their own as soon as they realize that your expectation of them is to be there on time and be ready to leave when their shift ends.

If he/she does become aggressive it could result in a physical confrontation which could lead to charges against the employee and perhaps against you as well if things get out of hand.

When to Approach

The best time to approach an employee about their behavior is not when you are in a hurry to leave and just want them out of the way. You should not be in a rush when dealing with this type of situation.

It is best if you can get away from your desk and go into another room to have the conversation. While it may seem easier for both of you if you can speak to them while sitting at your desk, it is better if you can walk away from your desk because it takes away some of the power that you have over them.

What to Say

"I've noticed that when it's time for you to leave, you seem to be reluctant to leave, and I'd like us to discuss why that is so."

The above statement is a good way of letting the employee know that you have noticed their behavior and may be having issues with it, but it is best if you can start by speaking about yourself or your feelings.

Final Tips

It is best if you can remain calm and not get into a confrontation with the employee. If they become aggressive because of your conversation, try to defuse their anger by reminding them that you are on their side and that you would like to be able to help them if they could just explain what is going on.

In most cases, this situation will resolve itself quickly once the employee realizes that they are expected to follow the rules and laws of the workplace. Most employees should have no problem with doing what is required of them and will leave when it is time to go home.

44. When it's Best to Let Them Go

One of the most difficult things a manager must do is fire a valued employee. When you fire someone, you are letting them down, and that's hard even for the best managers. For many managers, it's almost impossible.

The first thing to remember is that it's not about you, it's about them. If an employee can't do the job, then they have to go. The last thing you want is employees who are holding your business back or who are demoralizing their coworkers. Your credibility depends on getting rid of such people as soon as possible.

For whatever reason, some managers don't like firing people, and so they put it off longer than they should. It's better to fire someone immediately than to let them drag their feet and demoralize everyone in the office for weeks or months until they finally quit in disgust because no one is going to fire them.

Best Approach

First of all, keep in mind that you're not firing the employee because of their personality or because you don't like them. You're firing them because they are doing a poor job.

This is a very important distinction to make because it lets the employee know that they are still a valuable person and it isn't personal. You just don't want them to be part of your business anymore.

When to Approach

If an employee is a good person and their performance is lacking for any reason, you should sit down with them as soon as possible.

If they are a bad employee and their performance is poor, you shouldn't wait very long. If they are dragging their feet or demoralizing the other employees, then you need to intervene as soon as possible.

What to Say

"You're a good person and I don't like letting you go, but we can't keep you on staff because your performance has been lacking. This isn't just my decision, but several other people have had discussions with you about it."

"What is it that is making your job so difficult that no one wants to work with you? We've tried everything we could think of to work this out. Is there some way we can get you back on track, or do you not like this job anymore?"

"When is the best time for us to sit down one on one and discuss how we can resolve these issues? You deserve to have a face-to-face discussion about the situation instead of having everyone avoid talking to you about it."

"I'm sorry I have to let you go, but I just don't see any other option. If there were anything else, I could do, then I would consider it."

Final Tips

The key to firing an employee is to always treat them with respect. You should avoid blaming them or criticizing their personality. If you have an open relationship with your employees, they will be much more likely to understand why they are fired.

45. Discuss Reductions in Force with Employees

Tough times can cause many employees to lose direction. The reason for a reduction in force is something you need to discuss with the employees who will be affected.

A reduction in force is done to make a company more efficient by cutting some of the positions that are not producing as much as they could.

However, many companies go through this process for no other reason than to save money. The term "RIF" can create anxiety within all employees. It is important to communicate with your staff before and during this process if you want them to stay positive about the situation.

Best Approach

In a meeting with all employees that will be laid off, explain the situation and what the company is doing to ensure that the employees are placed in jobs that are still available within the company.

Explain how their severance package works and what type of benefits they will receive, such as health insurance. Some people may be upset that they must pay for their health insurance if they have been covered by the company all this time. However, remind them that many employers offer no coverage, and this is a good deal for them.

When to Approach

You can start to provide this information as soon as you know that a reduction in force will take place. You may want to do an exit interview with the employees that will be laid off. At this time, you can discuss the severance package and what role they played in the company. You also need to tell them about the job openings within the company.

What to Say

"We are doing some restructuring within the company, and unfortunately, several positions will be eliminated. I regret to inform you that your position is on the list. However, our goal is to find you another position within the company."

"I realize that this can be a difficult time for you and your family. We have a severance package that will help cushion the blow of not having a job right now. I will be happy to explain all of the details with you."

"We are currently looking for people who have your skill set and we would like to offer you an interview for one of these positions. If you are interested in returning to work at our company, please send me your resume."

Final Tips

Don't make promises that you cannot keep.

Do not argue with the employee about the decision to eliminate their job.

Be honest and upfront about everything you are doing for them.

Give them a clear path for getting back to work. This is important if your company is small and only has a couple of positions available. You want to assure them that there are options available for them.

46. Probationary Termination

The probationary period of your employees is a very important phase in the employee life cycle because it is a time that you get to know the real strengths and weaknesses of an employee. It is also a period when you can improve employees by giving them enough time in the organization.

This gives them a chance to adapt themselves to your company's work culture and to display their true potential.

Best Approach

It is very necessary that when you want to discuss probationary termination with an employee, you need to explain something positive about the concerned employee. This will make the discussion less tense and more fruitful. You should try to keep it short and simple by stating your reasons for the decision.

What to Say

"Due to the current situation of our company, we are going to let you go. We have been very happy with your work, and we are sorry that it has come to this."

Final Tips

The most important thing that you should remember is to be as positive as possible. This will help the employee to accept the decision and they will also be thankful to you for having a positive attitude.

You should also try to thank them for their time in your company and remind them that they were valuable employees.

You can also ask them if they have any questions or anything else that they want to discuss with you.

47. A Warning Notice

When working with employees, there are times when you must give a warning notice to an employee, which is referred to as a final warning. A final warning is usually given only after the employee has already received a written warning notice.

A final warning notice to an employee can be given when the issue of misconduct has been discussed in detail with the employee and after the employee has been given a chance to explain his or her side of the story. It is important that you do not give a final warning unless you have taken all measures to resolve the issue and ensure that your workers do not repeat their mistakes again. It will also depend on the nature of misconduct as well as how serious it is.

Best Approach

Give the employee a written warning notice. You must ensure that you give the employee a written warning notice as required by law.

Discuss with the employee in private. It is best that you discuss your concerns with the employee in private so that it is easier for him or her to open up and express his or her feelings. It is also important to ensure that you are not interrupted by other employees who may be eavesdropping on your conversation.

Discuss the misconduct. You should discuss the issue of misconduct in detail with the employee, and it is important to tell him or her why you are giving him or her a final warning. Some of the reasons for which a final warning can be given include constant tardiness, poor performance, and failure to follow instructions from superiors.

Suggest ways in which he/she can improve. After a discussion with the employee about his or her issues, you must ensure that you give him or her some advice on how he/she can correct his/her mistakes and improve his/her performance. You should also make sure that you offer support by providing resources such as training classes as well as counseling sessions, if necessary. This will help improve your relationship with your workers and they will also be motivated to improve their performance.

When to Approach

It is important that you do not give a final warning notice unless the misconduct has been discussed in detail with the employee and he or she has had a chance to defend himself or herself. If you have already given an employee a written warning notice and he or she continues to repeat the same mistake, then it is necessary that you give him or her a final warning notice.

What to Say

"I have given you a written warning notice before and I have discussed this matter with you in detail. I do not want to discuss this matter any further, but if you continue to repeat the same mistake, I will be forced to give you a final warning."

"As an employee, you must follow the instructions of your superior. If you fail to do so, I will have no other option but to give you a final warning notice."

"Since your performance has been below average for some time now, I am giving you a final warning notice. If your performance does not improve within one month, then I will have no other option but to terminate your employment."

Final Tips

It is important that you discuss with the employee about his or her performance and how his or her misconduct has affected the overall performance of your company.

If you feel that the misconduct has been done deliberately, then you can give him or her a final warning notice.

If you feel that the employee has not learned from his mistakes and continues to repeat them, then you must give him or her a final warning notice.

48. Making A Case for Voluntary Resignation

The rule of thumb in this regard is that you should make your case for the employee to choose voluntary resignation. This is because a voluntary resignation option is more favorable for both the employee and the organization than a forced exit.

When you force a person to resign from his or her job, you may not be able to save your image. You may be in trouble with law enforcement authorities if the person decides to retaliate by filing false complaints against your organization.

Best Approach

In this case, you need to be very careful not to hurt the dignity of the employee. The employee may feel insulted if he or she is forced to resign from his or her job. You must make sure that the employee understands that it is his or her decision and you have no say in this matter. You must also make sure that you do not insult the employee by making him or her feel like they are too incompetent for their job.

Make sure that there is no room for misinterpretation on your part while discussing the voluntary resignation options with the employee who is planning on resigning from work.

When to Approach

You should approach the employee to discuss voluntary resignation option when you are sure that he or she is planning to leave the job. You may not want to approach the employee on a Monday morning and ask him or her to resign from work due to a poor performance record.

What to Say

"The reason why I want to talk to you today is that I am getting complaints from your coworkers about your behavior. I want you to know that these are not the only complaints. Other employees have also complained about your behavior and performance. I would want you to think about resigning from work as an option for yourself. There is no shame in this matter. As per the law, you can choose to quit or resign from your job at any point in time without giving a reason for this decision."

"I am aware that you have put a lot of hard work into this job, but unfortunately, your performance has not been up to the mark. I can't provide feedback on this issue with you since I do not know what exactly has led to the decline in your productivity and output."

"I understand that it is hard for you to look for another job due to your financial obligations and commitments. This is why we should mutually agree upon a date as per which you would start preparing yourself to leave this organization."

"I would request you not to take any drastic step until we can sit together and discuss all possible options available in this case."

Final Tips

The employer should stress the fact that he or she does not want to force the employee to leave his or her job.

You need to make it clear that it is the employee who is planning on leaving, and you have no say in this matter.

You should also discuss the fact that there is no point in repaying any dues to the employee before he or she leaves his or her job.

49. Negotiating a Severance Package

This conversation is one you would rather avoid but feel you should have with a staff member. As you know, there are many reasons for one employee to ask for a severance package. It could be a company-wide layoff or a simple desire to leave your company. It is important to remember, that no matter the reason, the employee still has needs and rights under the law that must be addressed if you are going to ask him or her to leave.

Best Approach

The best way to handle this conversation is to provide the employee with a written severance agreement. This will lay out the terms of his or her severance package. You can make the agreement retroactive from the date of their choosing. The employee will have some time to consider the offer and discuss it with family members or a representative before making a final decision.

When to Approach

It is best to have this conversation in person to ensure that you can read the employee's reactions and body language. You will also be better able to focus on what is being said and make sure that the employee understands all information provided. Make sure you schedule enough time for this meeting so that you don't feel rushed or pressed for time.

What to Say

"I want to give you some time to think about this severance package. I'd like you to go home and talk it over with your family. I'll give you a call on Friday afternoon to see if you have questions or concerns. I want to make sure that you understand everything in this agreement before you make a final decision."

Final Tips

If the employee has questions regarding the agreement, it is your responsibility to answer them. If you have doubts about the employee's ability to understand the information, consider having a family member or friend present during the discussion.

It is important to remember that the employee is still an employee of the company until he or she signs the agreement and receives severance pay. In other words, it isn't time for celebratory parties just yet.

After a final decision has been made, you should go over the severance agreement one final time. Do not make any promises beyond what is stated in the agreement.

50. Verbal Acceptance of Resignation

Having a difficult conversation with employees about verbal acceptance of resignation is one of the most challenging conversations that a manager may have. It is challenging because if the manager fails to inform the employee in advance regarding their verbal acceptance of resignation, it may result in unfavorable outcomes for both the manager and the employee.

Best Approach

Review the conversation with the employee about the verbal acceptance of resignation and include what you said. Do not add anything at this point, just review it. Be sure that you are certain your employee understands what was discussed. It is important to keep in mind that verbal agreements can be legally binding, so if you are not sure if your employee understands what was said or if there are any misunderstandings, you need to discuss it further with them.

When to Approach

If you have not done so already, then it is important to schedule a meeting as soon as possible. Don't delay, because if you do, then your employee may be gone, and you may lose the opportunity to discuss the verbal resignation. Do not wait until the employee has given notice and quit to have this conversation, because it will be too late at that point.

What to Say

"I know that we both had a conversation about you resigning verbally, and I wanted to review that conversation with you so that we are both clear. Can you go back to the day when we had that conversation and tell me what you remember us saying?"

Final Tips

It is important to show your employee that you care about how they feel and what they are going through. Also, it is important to reassure them that you are willing to work with them through their transition and help them find a new job.

51. No-fault Layoff

Due to unforeseeable situations, firms may have to downsize their scale of employment due to various financial burdens and other management issues. In this situation, it can seem difficult to bring up the topic of unemployment for long-standing employees. It is the duty of the manager to make the employees aware of the situation and understand the desperate need for taking such actions. It is better to keep employees informed so that they can prepare themselves rather than keeping uninformed.

Best Approach

The tone of the meeting is very important. The manager should let the employee know that they are being considered for possible layoff because of the business situation and not because they are doing a bad job, do not fit in, or are not liked by management. The employee will need to be told that this is a company-wide economic situation and that it is out of their control.

When to Approach

The manager should approach the employee as soon as possible. The employee should be told as soon as possible that there is a possibility of them being laid off. It is important to have this discussion before they are actually laid off so that they can begin to look for a new job and so that they can start a job search earlier if necessary.

What to Say

"I am here to discuss the current business situation of the company. I am concerned about possible layoffs, but I do not know what the final decision will be. It is very important that you know that this is not your fault and it is not because you are not doing a good job or are a bad fit for the company."

Final Tips

The manager should make every effort to locate other jobs within the company or to relocate anyone who may need to move, but they should also make the employee aware that if a position cannot be located within the company, or if they decide not to relocate, they will receive severance packages as required by law.

52. Voluntary Layoff

Voluntary layoff is a very difficult discussion to have with an employee. It is one of the most difficult topics to discuss with an employee.

Voluntary layoff occurs when an employer asks a group of employees to accept a termination package voluntarily for short-term financial gains. Voluntary layoff is also known as Voluntary Separation Program (VSP) or Early Retirement Program (ERP). Employees who accept the offer are considered laid off from their jobs, and are entitled to salary and benefits for a period of time specified by the employer.

Best Approach

Be clear and concise. Before initiating the discussion, the manager needs to be able to explain the seriousness of the situation clearly and concisely. The manager needs to have a good understanding of the company's short-term financial goals and its long-term plans for growth.

The manager needs to outline how this decision is in the best interests of both the organization and employees. Then, he or she can explain how this layoff would help achieve this goal.

When to Approach

In a layoff situation, the manager may decide that the least disruptive time to have this discussion is when employees are in a group. This will help minimize the negative effects on each employee individually.

The manager should talk to each employee individually about his or her situation, especially if the employee has been with the organization for a long time.

What to Say

"In order to minimize the negative impacts on your life and career, I have decided to lay off a few people in a group. If you are one of those people, I will explain your situation in detail."

"As you know, our company has been facing some financial problems. These issues are very complex, and they involve a lot of factors. However, I can tell you that we have come up with a solution."

"We have to make some difficult decisions to continue achieving our long-term goals of growth and success."

"You may notice that some of your colleagues will be leaving soon. Therefore, I need to talk about what will happen next."

"Based on the information you provided me earlier this year during the annual review process, we have decided that you are the employee who needs to leave the organization right now."

Final Tips

The manager should provide as much information as possible about the benefits of accepting the voluntary layoff offer and why it is in the best interest of both the organization and employees.

If the employee asks why he or she was chosen, do not say you were looking for a reason to fire him or her. Rather, explain that this decision was made based on the needs of the organization. If you are unsure what to say, avoid using phrases such as "it is not personal" or "you are not a good fit."

53. Reduction in Work Hours

This is a difficult conversation to have with an employee. This conversation is likely to be unpleasant. You may think that the employee might get upset and angry and blame you for not supporting him/her in his career development. However, it is necessary to have the conversation to prevent employees from being unhappy and stressed out at work.

Best Approach

The best approach to avoid resentment and anger is to tell your employee that you are concerned about the impact of the job on his/her family and personal life. You can tell him/her you feel it would be better for both him/her and the organization if he/she worked a reduced number of hours.

You can make it clear to the employee that you will support him/her through his/her career development. You will discuss with his/her manager what alternative arrangements can be made for him/her at work. You will also help him/her look for other jobs within or outside the organization that could be a better fit for his/her current situation.

When to Approach

This conversation should be approached as soon as you notice that the employee's work patterns are affecting his/her personal life and career.

What to Say

"I'm concerned about how much work you are doing. It's affecting your personal life and your career. I don't want to see you unhappy at work or leaving the organization. I care about you as a person and as an employee. I want to look at what we can do to help your career development and make sure that both of us are happy."

Final Tips

Have a discussion with the employee's manager to find out if any alternative work arrangements could be made for him/her. Discuss options and scenarios that would give the employee some flexibility in his/her work hours. You can also help the employee find another job that would be a better fit for him/her.

54. Disbanding A Team

Whether it's an individual contributor or the entire team, there are times when you will face the issue of handing out pink slips. There are many arguments against this, but there are also numerous situations when it is inevitable. So as a manager, how do we handle this?

Best Approach

After breakups, marriages, and divorces, most people need lots of time to heal. The same is true for employees who are let go from their jobs. When you must lay someone off, it's important to give them sufficient time to search for new employment. That means not placing them on the street immediately after they leave the office. This doesn't mean that they can't be contacted by potential employers before being officially terminated (assuming you have an employee handbook).

When to Approach

My recommendation is that you pull the employee into your office and have a very honest and open discussion with them. Let them know exactly why they are being let go and try to give them a sense of the business environment. While it's not easy, it's important to be honest with them. You can tell them that they are a hard worker, but the company is not in a position to hold onto employees for the long term.

What to Say

"Jim, you've always been a hard worker, but unfortunately we're not in a position to hold onto employees for the long term. Even though you have been with us for several years, we now need to let you go. You're entitled to some severance pay, and I would be happy to walk you through the paperwork."

Final Tips

Try to keep your emotions in check. It's a very difficult time for both you and the employee, but if you can remain objective, it will make the process a little easier for all parties involved.

55. Workforce Restructuring

This is a difficult conversation to have with an employee. The company is laying off 30% of the workforce in the next six months. The company must do this because of the sudden downturn in business (30% decline in sales). Many employees will be required to leave the organization but there will be no job opportunities for them in other companies.

Best Approach

The best approach is to have a one-on-one discussion with the employee and explain what is happening in the organization. Let them know that this restructuring is being done because of the sudden downturn in sales and it will affect everyone.

When to Approach

If the employee is not aware of the restructuring, you should approach them immediately so that they know what is going on.

The best time to approach the employee is during their lunch break. You can have a nice informal discussion over lunch and tell them that some restructuring will happen in the company and it will affect everyone.

If the employee is aware of the situation, then do not waste time and directly approach them.

What to Say

"Hi, Ben, I need to have a word with you to discuss some important issues. There is a possibility that we will have to restructure the workforce in the company, and it will affect everyone. I really do not want to do this, but the sales are down by 30% and there is no choice left for us. I am not going to lay off employees, but we might have to let go of some employees."

"We are restructuring because of the sudden downturn in sales, and it will affect everyone. We are not laying off employees, but we might have to let go of some employees. This is hard for me as well but I do not have any other option as this is what is needed right now."

"I am sorry that this has happened."

Final Tips

Do not beat around the bush and be frank with the employee. Do not be afraid to have these difficult conversations.

Do not hide anything from the employee. Be honest and upfront with them.

The best way to handle this situation is with kindness and empathy. Show them that you care about their well-being and you are there for them as their manager.

Be honest about what is happening in the organization and do not hide anything from them. This will only complicate things for both of you in the future if they ever find out that you hid something from them at this point in time when they needed your support more than ever.

56. Relocation

People who are relocated will face a lot of problems. Many employees are unable to accept the relocation, and, in turn, they must move from their present companies. Many employees dispute with their managers and feel that they are not getting proper attention from them. If you are in such a situation, you can refer to this book and learn how to deal with such situations.

Best Approach

In general, relocation is a common thing and happens at many places. Employees can't accept the relocation in their personal lives. Therefore, you should remain calm and try to explain to them that it is a part of their job and has been done before by many employees. You can also ask them if they are willing to relocate, as it would only be beneficial for them in the long run.

When to Approach

You should discuss relocation with the employee when you feel that they are not properly accepting the proposal. If you do it during the time of their joining, then it might create some issues and they may move out from your company. It is better to talk to them when you feel that it is necessary.

What to Say

"We are having a new office building, and we are moving there so that we can provide you with better facilities and services. We will try to minimize your cost by providing you with the assistance of the relocation company."

"We are expanding our business, and one of the ways to do so is to move our existing employees to the new office. We have decided to relocate you to the new office. If you are willing, then we can discuss this in further detail."

Final Tips

You should always keep in mind that the decision of relocation is only up to the employee, and it is not binding for them. You should try to convince them as much as possible, and explain the benefits of moving to the new office. If they are willing, you can proceed with the relocation process.

Workplace Politics

This chapter provides a few examples of the workplace politics that exist in today's workplace. It also provides a few tips on how to deal with those who are strong in the political scene while at the same time giving solid examples of how to handle those who may be "sucking up" to their superiors.

57. The "Queen Bee" Syndrome

The queen bee syndrome is a natural tendency among women to be critical of other women. It stems from an instinctive desire to maintain power and be dominant in the workplace. This is a difficult behavior for the manager to confront and discuss. However, if it is not addressed, it can become a serious problem at work.

Best Approach

When dealing with an employee who is displaying queen bee syndrome, it is important to confront the behavior and discuss the impact it can have on the team. The best approach is to remain calm and open with the employee. Choose a private place when discussing this issue, so that you can speak freely.

When to Approach

This can be a difficult issue to address, but it is important to address it sooner rather than later. If the behavior does not change, it can have serious consequences. The behavior can also affect other employees and cause problems for the team.

What to Say

"I've noticed that you are very critical of other employees at work. I'm concerned about this behavior because it can hurt your coworkers and the team. For example, if you are critical of one employee, it can make them feel bad and affect their performance. Also, the rest of the team might not be able to work effectively with that person because they are afraid to try new things."

"I would like to discuss a way that you can work through these issues with other employees without being so critical."

Final Tips

When working with an employee who is displaying the queen bee syndrome, it is important to be open and honest. It is also important that you show you are concerned about the behavior being displayed.

58. Issue of Employee Favoritism

One of the most difficult of all employee issues is the matter of how to deal with employees who exhibit favoritism. Favoritism is an issue that can arise in any business setting, whether it's a small company or a large corporation.

Best Approach

The best approach to this issue is to be direct and to the point. Employees who participate in favoritism are usually causing more harm than good and making the situation worse by creating a negative culture within the workplace.

When to Approach

You should approach your employee when you become aware of the situation. Do not wait for the issue to resolve itself because it will not. If you don't deal with it immediately, the issue will get worse, and the employee will continue to make poor decisions in favor of one person or group.

What to Say

"Jane, I'm aware of the fact that you have been showing favoritism to Michael. This is creating an issue within the company, and I will not allow it to continue."

Final Tips

If you are having trouble with this issue, try to have someone in the company, such as a consultant, help you with the conversation.

If this issue is causing a great deal of stress within your business, consider hiring an HR consultant to help you work through it.

59. Complaints Against the Manager

When an employee is unhappy with the manager, it is not a pleasant situation for either party. Unfortunately, there are times when a manager feels that he or she has been treated unfairly by an employee or a group of employees. It really is not as easy as it seems to work through this type of situation.

Best Approach

First you must realize that the employee is going to be upset about something. You should tell him/her that you understand, that this is not personal and that you would appreciate it if they could tell you what is bothering them.

When to Approach

The best time to approach the employee is when he/she is not upset. If the employee is upset, let them vent, and then approach them later.

What to Say

"I understand that something is bothering you. Please share with me what it is."

"If there is something I need to do to make the situation better, please let me know."

"Unless you tell me what the problem is, I will not be able to help you."

Final Tips

If the employee is upset, let him/her vent, and then approach them later. Never try to resolve the issue when the employee is upset. You will not be able to have a productive conversation.

60. Gossiping About Personal Damaging Information

When an employee is caught spreading rumors about someone's personal life it can be a difficult situation for the manager to handle. This type of gossip is always damaging, but when it happens in the workplace, the damage can be particularly serious.

Best Approach

Because this type of gossip is always damaging, it is important to take the time to talk with the employee who has been spreading it. This is particularly true if the gossip has gotten back to upper management, or if it has affected morale within the workforce.

When to Approach

You can wait until you have a little more information before approaching the person who has been spreading gossip, but if it is affecting the workplace in a significant way, it will be important to address it as soon as possible.

What to Say

"Mary, I know that you have been talking about Jane's personal life. I realize how difficult it is to be a close friend and not gossip. However, this information is damaging to the workplace and has to stop."

Final Tips

It is important that you have a plan worked out with upper management before you approach the employee. You should know what action you will take if the situation does not improve. Depending on the situation, you may need to remove the employee from the workplace or even let them go.

61. Flattering Supervisors

Managers will have to face this issue of how to handle employees who flatter their supervisors. It is an important issue because if the manager does not handle it well, the manager could end up in a losing situation.

When an employee flirts with a supervisor, he or she is putting themselves in a position to get the rewards that they want in exchange for sexual favors. This is something that most managers are not willing to do, and therefore they need to know how to handle it when it happens.

Best Approach

The best approach for the manager is to tell the employee that the flirting is inappropriate and that it must stop. The manager must be direct and clear in telling the employee that they are not willing to flirt back.

When to Approach

This is an important topic to discuss with employees because it can happen in any business. Most managers will have to deal with it at some point, so they need to be prepared for it.

When the employee is flirting with the supervisor, the manager should tell them that they are inappropriate and must stop immediately. If the employee continues this behavior, the manager should approach them again and tell them that if they do not stop flirting, there will be consequences.

What to Say

"I need you to stop flirting with the supervisor. It is inappropriate, and it needs to stop. If you continue this behavior, there will be consequences."

Final Tips

When managers deal with these issues, they must remain professional. They should not get into any kind of a power struggle with the employee. It is important to be firm and direct but not to make threats. The best approach is to let the employee know that they are doing something unacceptable in your workplace, and that if it continues, there will be consequences.

62. Stealing Work Credit

If an employee is stealing work credit, it is a serious situation that should be discussed with the employee in a business manner. The manager should try to discover the reasons for the actions and discuss them with the employee.

Best Approach

The manager should discuss the relationship with the employee and try to find out why they are stealing work credit. The manager should discuss with the employee in a private setting, such as in a conference room or office.

When to Approach

The manager should approach the employee when they are alone, away from other people, and when the discussion will be confidential. The manager will need to approach the employee before a situation gets out of control and someone is hurt, or a major problem is created that may get worse if not addressed.

What to Say

"How are you doing? I have been noticing that you are taking credit for the work of others, and I wanted to talk to you about that."

"I know that it is important to take work credit when it is due, but I have noticed that you have been doing this a lot, and I wanted to talk with you about this."

"I want to make sure that we are all on the same page about what we do here. Can we sit down and discuss some ways to get us back on track?"

Final Tips

The manager should discuss the issue with the employee in a business manner. They should try to keep it simple and to the point. The manager should have guidelines and examples of what actions are acceptable and unacceptable.

Afterward, follow up with the employee on how they feel about what was discussed. If things seem to be okay, then the manager can move on with their work, but if things get out of hand, then they will need to address them again.

63. Sabotaging Coworkers

An employee may complain that one of his coworkers is deliberately sabotaging him. The manager must first determine if the complaints are justified. This may be difficult since the complaint is usually made by an employee who does not get along with other employees. It is important to determine if there is a pattern of sabotage, or if it happened just once. If there is a pattern, then you should talk with both parties. If it happened just once and the employee was not successful in accomplishing his sabotage, then it should be handled as a simple misunderstanding between the two employees.

Best Approach

If there is a pattern of sabotage, then you should talk with both parties. If there was a single occurrence, then you should talk to the employee who sabotaged his coworker. You should talk to both employees about their relationship and how they can work together better.

When to Approach

Ideally, you should have a talk with the employee after the problem has occurred. If the situation is still ongoing or has escalated, you should talk to them immediately. If it is a single occurrence and it has not escalated, you should talk to them the next time they come to you about the issue.

What to Say

"Mike, I have received several complaints about you from your coworkers. They say that you are sabotaging their work. They also feel you are not doing your fair share of the work."

"I've talked to some of your coworkers, and they say that they feel like you are sabotaging their work. They also believe that you are not doing your fair share of the work."

"Mike, I've heard about several incidents where it sounds like you purposely sabotaged the work of other employees. Both employees were very upset by what happened."

"I talked to one of your coworkers who says he feels like he is being sabotaged by you for no reason. He says it has been happening for a few months now. I talked to another one of your coworkers and she says that you have been deliberately trying to sabotage her work, but she was successful in preventing this from happening."

Final Tips

You must talk with both employees about their relationship. Talk to them about how they can work together better.

Risky Romance

There are several reasons why managers find it difficult to discuss these issues with employees. Firstly, it is not always easy to differentiate between what is a personal relationship and what is work-related. Secondly, the issues involved are often very sensitive and personal to the individuals involved. Lastly, there may be some concern about how the matter will be handled if it becomes public knowledge.

This chapter considers the issues of employees who have a relationship with each other. It is not always easy for managers to address this because the issue may be a sensitive one.

64. Inappropriate Romantic Relationship with Another Employee

This is a very delicate conversation to have with an employee. The manager needs to be tactful and gentle when having this conversation; if not, the employee will feel insulted. This conversation cannot take place in a public area or near other employees as this may give the impression that the manager is trying to embarrass the employee. This is a private matter and should be handled as such.

Best Approach

Start the conversation by explaining that you need to discuss some confidential information with the employee. You then explain that you are required by law to report any relationship between employees, whether consensual or not. You should ask the employee if they have any questions and then move on to the next topic.

When to Approach

This conversation should be approached when it is observed that an employee is inappropriately spending a lot of time with another employee, or when the manager sees the employee constantly texting, emailing, or calling another employee.

What to Say

"I have been made aware of an inappropriate relationship between you and another employee. I am required by law to report this relationship. I need to know if this is an ongoing situation or if it was a one-time occurrence."

"I am sure you are aware of the policies that we have in place regarding relationships between employees. This is a very serious issue, and we do not take it lightly."

Final Tips

Be professional and maintain a calm demeanor. Give the employees time to respond to your questions and be sure to ask them if they have any questions about your concerns.

It is important to remember that you may not have all the facts regarding this situation, so it is best to wait until you do before making any decisions regarding the employee. Doing so will help prevent you from making a hasty decision that could be detrimental to the company in the long run.

65. Inappropriate Romantic Relationship with a Client

This section discusses the situations where a manager or senior professional should have a difficult discussion with an employee about inappropriate romantic relationships with a client. These situations can be a violation of the company's policy and ethics or can cause major damage to the organization if not handled on time.

Best Approach

The best approach is to have a one-on-one discussion with the employee about the situation. The manager or senior professional should calmly discuss the matter so that the employee does not feel intimidated.

To start with, explain why you are having the discussion and ensure that you are not blaming him or her for doing something wrong. You must make sure to understand his or her side of the story as well. Try to come up with an agreement on how to handle the situation moving forward.

When to Approach

If you are a manager and you find out that your employee has been involved in an inappropriate romantic relationship with a client, you must discuss this matter on time. If the situation is not attended to, it can cause major damage to the organization.

What to Say

"I have noticed an inappropriate romantic relationship between you and your client. I would like to understand the situation from your end before we decide on a way forward."

Final Tips

The manager should understand the situation from the employee's point of view as well. The manager should make sure that the employee feels comfortable in sharing his or her side of the story. It is also important that the manager understands the situation from his or her own point of view as well and decides on a way forward after listening to all sides.

66. Public Display of Affection in the Workplace

This is one of the most sensitive topics that a manager must deal with. The most common questions are: how should a manager deal with an employee's public display of affection, and how should a manager approach this topic?

Best Approach

The best approach to deal with this is to be direct and make the employee understand that it is an unprofessional behavior. The manager needs to tell the employee how his/her behavior affects teamwork and productivity in a negative manner.

When to Approach

The manager should refrain from approaching employees during office hours. The best time would be when they are not in the office. The manager can approach the employee during lunchtime or after work hours and talk to him/her individually.

What to Say

"Hey, Peter. I have noticed you and your girlfriend spending a lot of time together in the office. I think it is affecting the work performance of the team members. The behavior is unprofessional and should be avoided. It is better to meet outside the office and not in a public place. I am sure you will understand."

Final Tips

It is important that the manager talks to the employee in a calm and composed manner.

The manager should also explain how such behavior affects productivity and teamwork.

The manager should make sure that he keeps his explanation simple and clear. The employee needs to understand professionally the problems behind this behavior.

67. Unwanted Romantic Advances from an Employee's Coworker

In this section, we will learn how to handle the situation where a manager receives a complaint from an employee that they are being harassed by a coworker. This is a common scenario that occurs daily in the workplace. It causes concern for the manager and often results in disciplining the offending employee.

Best Approach

This situation needs to be handled in a tactful manner that does not result in damaging the relationship with the employee who is being harassed. This is a difficult issue for the manager and one that needs to be handled with care.

When to Approach

The manager should approach the employee who complains about being harassed by a coworker. This employee will usually be more willing to talk to you about this issue since they are the one who has had to endure unwanted attention from someone they work with. Be careful not to approach this situation too early, as it may seem that you are overreacting to the situation.

What to Say

"I am concerned about this issue and I want to address the matter with you both."

"I want you to know that I will not tolerate any harassment in the workplace. If anyone is making you feel uncomfortable, I want to know about it so that we can deal with it in a professional manner."

"I need for you both to agree that whatever is said between us will remain confidential and that there will be no repercussions for talking about this situation."

"I need you both to understand that neither of you is at fault here—this is a mutual problem that we need to deal with together. I am not here to reprimand either of you—I just want to make sure all parties are comfortable in the workplace, and that we do not have any issues like this again."

Final Tips

Make sure you let the employee who is being harassed know that you will help him/her cope with this problem as well.

Do not assume that the employee who is being harassed is overreacting or is making a big deal out of nothing.

Show this employee that you care about him/her and his/her feelings by listening to him/her and letting him/her know that you will help him/her resolve this issue.

Sexual Harassment Issues

Sexual harassment is a common issue that can arise in the workplace, and while it is prohibited under federal law, many companies choose to have a more stringent policy. Sexual harassment can take many forms, and most of the issues related to sexual harassment can be addressed using the policy and procedures outlined in this chapter.

68. An Employee Making Sexual Comments

A manager should never ignore an employee's sexual behavior or comments. This may be a manager's first experience with a sexual behavior complaint and can cause the manager to fumble through an uncomfortable conversation. Sexual and inappropriate comments can interfere with the work environment.

Best Approach

The manager should approach the employee with a matter-of-fact tone. It is important to state what the employee said that was inappropriate, and then allow the employee to respond. The manager should also explain how it was inappropriate so that the employee understands why this behavior is unacceptable.

When to Approach

The manager should approach the employee as soon as possible after hearing of the behavior. The manager should not wait until it becomes an issue. The employee will be more likely to change their behavior if they do not feel that they are being singled out.

What to Say

"I overheard you make a sexual comment to a coworker. I am not sure if you did that intentionally or if it just slipped out. I would like to discuss this with you in private."

"I am concerned that your comments may be inappropriate in the workplace. We have strict sexual harassment policies here at _____, and sexual comments may violate these policies."

"What is your understanding of sexual harassment?"

"I am suggesting that you stop doing this because it is not acceptable in our company. Do you understand why?"

Final Tips

The manager should explain to the employee that their sexual behavior is not appropriate in the workplace. The manager should also explain how the employee's behavior may be violating company sexual harassment policies.

69. Making Sexual Advances on Employees

Managers are responsible for making the decisions that affect their employees in the workplace. This includes deciding what to do when an employee makes unwanted sexual advances toward another employee. As a manager, you must take it upon yourself to solve these issues and make sure they don't happen again.

Best Approach

In a situation like this, you must act quickly and decisively. You must first address the issue with the person making the advances, either in private or in front of other employees. Depending on the severity of what is being said or done, you may want to remove yourself and the employee from your group for this discussion.

It's important to remember that no one can force another person to have sex with them. It's important that you drill this into your employees' minds, so they understand their actions are inappropriate and unacceptable. If necessary, you may want to remind them that they can be fired for such behavior.

You should then move on to speak with the other employee who was made uncomfortable by this behavior, as well as any other employees who may have witnessed it. You should let them know how unacceptable these actions are and how you will handle them from here on out.

When to Approach

You should approach this topic with the offending employee as soon as you notice the behavior change. You may also want to approach them if you see another employee who is uncomfortable with their actions.

What to Say

"I've noticed an increase in your sexual behavior around other employees. I need to remind you that this is unacceptable. All employees should feel comfortable and safe in the workplace, and you need to keep that in mind."

"I don't expect you to change your entire personality, but there are certain behaviors that can intimidate or make another employee feel uncomfortable. I don't want anyone to feel unsafe here, and I need you to be aware of that."

"I will not tolerate this behavior any longer. If it continues, I may have no choice but to fire you."

"You should also be aware that if you do this outside of work, it could damage the company's reputation or put its image in jeopardy. You should be aware that you are a representative of the company, and your conduct reflects on us."

Final Tips

Keep your tone neutral and calm. You should never raise your voice or sound frustrated when you're talking to this employee. You're the manager, and you need to show them that you are the boss and in charge.

Repeat yourself as necessary. Be sure to clearly state that these actions aren't appropriate and will not be tolerated.

70. Unwitting Sexual Harassment

Any sexual harassment that occurs in a workplace is extremely difficult for the manager to discuss with the employee. Even when the employee is unaware that there has been any harassment, it is still very difficult to explain why the manager needs to discuss this sensitive subject with the employee.

Best Approach

This discussion should only be held in private, and the employee should be advised that they have the right to speak with a representative from their union or Human Resources. The manager must be very sensitive to the employee and how they will react to this discussion. The manager is advised not to discuss details of the sexual harassment and should only focus on the impact of this behavior on the company and other employees.

When to Approach

This discussion should take place as soon as possible after the manager is made aware of the sexual harassment. The manager must inform the employee that he or she is being discussed in a meeting and what will be discussed. The employee must be informed that this discussion will not take place unless they agree to attend.

What to Say

"I am very sorry to have to discuss this with you, but I have been asked by the company to discuss your behavior with you. The company is concerned that your behavior is not appropriate, and other employees are uncomfortable around you. The company has received complaints that you are using inappropriate language, sexually touching other employees, or taunting other employees with your actions. We need to discuss why this behavior is inappropriate and how it affects the company."

"You have every right to call a representative from your union or Human Resources if you wish."

"If you feel that this issue is too sensitive for me to discuss with you, I will be more than happy to allow one of these representatives to address it with you."

Final Tips

The manager should avoid the temptation to discuss all the details of the harassment. The manager should only focus on the impact of the behavior on the company and other employees.

The employee must be made aware that they can call a representative from their union or Human Resources at any time if they feel this discussion is too difficult to handle alone.

71. Molestation

The situation is one where a manager has an employee who has been accused of sexual molestation. The situation is one where the employee has admitted to the crime. The manager is concerned about the situation and needs to be able to discuss it with other employees of the organization.

Best Approach

The best approach is to allow the employee to share what they did wrong and why they did it. This will allow the manager to be able to talk about the issue with others without violating the privacy of the employee.

When to Approach

The best time to approach this employee is immediately after the event happened and just before the employee returns to work. This will allow the manager to question the employee about what occurred, how they feel about it, and what they want to do about it in the future.

What to Say

"I have to talk with you about an issue that has come up at work. There is an allegation that you molested another employee. I must be very careful, as every employee in this company is innocent until proven guilty. I also have to be very careful not to violate your privacy and keep the information confidential."

"I do not believe that you have done anything wrong, but I need to know what happened."

"I need you to tell me everything that happened. Then I will know what I can say about it."

"Did you do this? If you did, then I need to know why."

"You are doing the right thing by telling me. It will help me keep your privacy intact while allowing others to know that this happened."

Final Tips

The manager should make sure that the employee feels that they did the right thing by telling them. The employee should also be encouraged to tell other employees about what happened. This will prevent rumors from spreading.

72. Peeping Tom

Peeping Tom is a real problem in the office. The employee accused of being a Peeping Tom does not admit his deviant behavior, but he is always looking into one of the ladies' rooms. He says that he is just looking to make sure no one is stealing office supplies from the supply room.

Best Approach

The best approach to handle this problem is to confront the employee about it. The best time to confront him is when he is not in the middle of doing his job. The manager should ask the employee if he has been peeping in the ladies' room.

When to Approach

The best time to approach the employee is when he is not in the middle of doing his job.

What to Say

"I have seen you peeping into the ladies' room."

"Everyone at work has been told about your habit."

"We need to talk about your inappropriate behavior."

Final Tips

If the employee denies he is peeping into the ladies' room, then ask him why his eyes are always turning toward the ladies' room every time someone goes inside.

If the employee still denies, tell him you have been informed that he likes to peep at women after they have used the toilet. Tell him that everyone at work knows about his dirty habit, and if he does not stop soon, you will report him to your superiors and his boss.

73. Stalking

Stalking is a very serious issue for many people. For those who have been victimized, the problems associated with stalking can be extreme and traumatic. Some stalkers do not stop their harassment until the person being stalked changes jobs or moves out of state. If an employee has been being stalked, it is important that you are aware of the circumstances and that you take the appropriate action.

Best Approach

As a manager, you should treat the situation just as you would if it were any other harassment concern. However, since stalking is not a crime that is directly called for in the workplace, it may be difficult to know how to handle the situation. The best approach is to use your common sense and investigate the situation. This will involve talking to the stalker and the employee who is being stalked.

When to Approach

Many managers are told that they must wait until the behavior becomes physical before they can do anything. However, this is not true. As soon as you become aware of the situation, you should begin to investigate it. Depending on the circumstances, you may need to meet with the stalker and/or the employee being stalked within 24 hours of being notified of the problem.

What to Say

"James, I have received a complaint from Jane that you are sending her a lot of emails. I am wondering if there is some misunderstanding."

"Jane, I have received a complaint from James that you are sending him a lot of emails. He says that it is causing him some problems and he is concerned about your intentions."

"Jane, I would like to meet with you to discuss James' complaint. Can you come in on Monday?"

Final Tips

Do not ask for proof of harassment. You may imply this, but do not directly ask for proof of harassment because it may force the victim to come up with evidence that they might not have.

Do not rush the situation. Do not try to pressure either employee into deciding before it is appropriate to make one.

If either employee tells you of any physical contact, report this to your company's security department immediately.

74. Claims of Rape

It's not uncommon for a business to receive a call from someone alleging that a member of the company's workforce has raped them. Human Resources departments at companies are often not prepared for such accusations, and they often land in the hands of an unprepared manager.

Best Approach

When the employee is accused of raping someone, it is important to keep an open mind and listen carefully without jumping to conclusions. Make sure that your response shows that you are taking the allegation seriously and that you are not going to blame the accuser for coming forward with it.

Remember that there is a big difference between believing an accuser and believing that what they said was true. In cases where there have been no witnesses or evidence, it is important not to make any assumptions about what happened.

When to Approach

When you receive the allegation from the person who has brought it up, it is important to decide whether you will approach the employee or wait for them to come to you. If you are a manager, and an employee has brought up an accusation with you, you may choose to approach them directly.

If someone else brings up the issue, or if your company is contacted directly by a third party about it, it may be best not to approach the accused employee directly, but to let them come to you. If the accuser is someone who works for you, it may be a good idea to have a designated manager handle the situation instead.

If the accuser is someone who does not work for you, such as a client or vendor, it may be best not to approach the accused employee directly at all. Instead, your company's legal department may want to handle it. You should also consult with your company's Human Resources department if you're in doubt about how best to proceed.

What to Say

"I want to make sure that you feel safe in your interactions at work. I am concerned about what you have told me, and I want you to know that it will be handled."

"I understand that this is very difficult for you, and I want you to know that I'm glad that you're comfortable coming to me with this."

"I realize that this can be a sensitive issue, and I am committed to handling it with care. Let me know if there's anything else you need from me at this time."

Final Tips

If the accuser is a third party or if they do not work for you, it is important to handle the situation delicately and by your company's harassment policy. Don't make any assumptions about what has happened, and don't blame the accuser for coming forward.

It is best to let your company's Human Resources department handle this issue. You should consult with them in advance of approaching the accused employee if possible, to ensure that you are following your company's policies and procedures during the process.

Performance Issues

For some managers, it is easier to deal with firing an employee than it is to deal with performance issues. It's not that the manager doesn't care about the employee; it's just that if a performance issue is handled effectively, the manager and employee will both benefit.

If the problem isn't addressed, neither party wins. The employee won't improve and may fail in the job and/or leave for another opportunity. The manager will lose productivity and credibility with his or her boss and colleagues, as well as waste time dealing with a problem that could have been resolved before any damage was done.

75. Employee Performance is Slipping

An employee who is slacking off or not performing at the expected levels can be a huge problem for a manager. It can be difficult to tell an employee they are slipping in performance, and it can be even more difficult for the employee to accept your feedback. The key to having any sort of successful conversation is to ensure that both you and your employee feel respected and heard, regardless of how the conversation goes.

Best Approach

Make sure that you take the time to get to know your employee on a personal level. Try to avoid any sort of group meeting when possible. Make sure that you both have a place where you can sit comfortably and think clearly, and take the time to make sure that you are listening to what they have to say. This will help you avoid jumping to conclusions or making assumptions, which may make the situation worse.

When to Approach

You should approach the employee when you are sure they are slacking off. Avoid jumping to conclusions and always make sure that you have a solid reason before approaching the employee. Also, only approach the employee when you are able to have this conversation, not when there is a problem with the time you have available for your employees or with their schedule.

What to Say

"I have noticed that you have been struggling to perform to the best of your abilities lately. I am here to help you do as well as you can and want to discuss how we can get back on track."

"I know that sometimes it can be hard to take feedback, but I am always here for any questions or concerns that you may have."

Final Tips

If you have a particularly large group of employees, it may be easier to hold a meeting where everyone can get together and discuss their problems. Make sure you focus on the specific problems that your employee has and avoid generalizing their performance.

76. Poor Work Quality

The work quality of many employees in organizations is below par. Poor work quality is not a very positive attribute of an employee. Work quality can have a huge impact on the organization, and it can also influence the other employees in the organization.

Best Approach

To discuss this matter with the employee, it is advised that the manager should meet the employee individually for a one-on-one discussion, preferably in a private place and not in public, and discuss the issue casually.

When to Approach

It is essential to approach the employee after the manager has seen enough evidence of poor work quality.

What to Say

"I've noticed that your work quality is not very good. What is the problem that I can help you with to improve your work quality? Are you under any kind of pressure at home or at work that is affecting your work? Are you having any problems with your colleagues or managers? Is there anything else that is affecting your work quality?"

Final Tips

In this discussion, it is very important to keep a positive approach. This is because an employee might feel disheartened or embarrassed if the manager takes a negative approach and blames them for poor work quality.

The manager must understand that this poor work quality can be triggered by some issues such as the manager, stress, or maybe other problems. Therefore, it is important for the manager to keep a positive note when discussing with the employee.

77. Poor Time Management Skills

There are many reasons why a person has poor time management skills, and why he or she is not able to be on time. The person may have a problem with his or her biological clock and therefore cannot manage the time. It may also be an issue of self-discipline, where the person is not able to get started on tasks when they begin the workday. Then some do not have the self-discipline to stop doing something after a set time.

Best Approach

While it is a difficult conversation to have, the best approach is to be direct and to the point. You should first start the discussion by explaining what the issue is. Tell him or her about how you have noticed this problem in several instances, and how it affects the entire team. You should also explain that you need to discuss this with him or her, rather than confronting him or her in front of his peers.

When to Approach

This is a conversation that you should approach only after you have given him or her time to improve the situation. You should give him or her an extended period, and then observe his or her behavior to see if there is any improvement. You should also approach this type of discussion only when it is necessary, and not at every instance where he or she arrives late.

What to Say

"I have noticed that you are frequently late to meetings, and it is affecting the team. I have observed that there seem to be some issues with your time management skills, and I would like to discuss this with you."

"I need your help on this issue because it will affect not only your performance but also the performance of the team."

"If you are unable to improve your time management skills in a way that is acceptable for both of us, then we may need to take further action."

Final Tips

If he or she does not see the issue as you do, you should explain that it is not about one meeting or two, but about the overall impact on the team.

You should also explain that this is a long-term issue that may have to be addressed in other ways if he or she does not improve.

You can also suggest that you both agree to set up a schedule for this employee to keep track of his or her time during a month, and then review the data together. This will help them understand how they spend their time outside of work as well.

78. Employee Is Not Meeting Goals or Deadlines

This is a very common problem as an employer, and most often the manager will feel the pressure from the employee to give them more time to meet their goals or deadlines. The manager should never allow this, as it will lead to work being done at the last minute and quality will suffer.

Best Approach

You should sit down with the employee and discuss your concerns. Explain to them that you have noticed they are not meeting their deadlines and you want to help make sure they meet their goals. You want to be sure they are on track with the deadlines that they have been assigned to meet.

When to Approach

Ideally, this should be discussed at the end of each month after the employee has had time to complete their tasks for the month. The manager should sit down with them at the end of each month and discuss what they are working on. It is best to handle this discussion over lunch or coffee so that there is no pressure on the employee.

What to Say

"John, I noticed that you haven't been meeting your deadlines and you have been asking for more time to complete tasks. What can I do to help?"

"John, we have been talking about this for the last few months. I am concerned that my deadlines are not being met by you, and we are starting to miss our quarterly goals. What can we do to make sure this doesn't happen again?"

"John, I noticed that you haven't been meeting your deadlines, and you have been asking for more time to complete tasks. We have had a conversation before about this issue, and it is still happening. What can we do to make sure this doesn't happen again?"

Final Tips

It is important when speaking with employees about their lack of performance, or missing deadlines, that they don't get defensive or upset. Any employee should feel free to come forward with any issues they may be having at work or home. These kinds of conversations should be handled with care so as not to offend your employee.

79. Employee Not Performing Up to Expectations

It is never easy, when you must discuss with an employee that their performance is not up to the mark. You have a responsibility as a manager to let the employees know if they are not performing up to your expectations.

Best Approach

The best approach is to always have an open discussion with the employee. Make them aware that you will be discussing their performance. Don't sugarcoat it; let them know the issues that are affecting their performance.

When to Approach

You should hold a meeting with the employee as soon as you notice a performance issue.

If it is a small performance issue, one meeting should be sufficient to resolve the problem. If the issue is extensive, or if you are concerned that the employee will not perform up to your expectations, then you should hold multiple meetings with the employee.

What to Say

"I have noticed a few issues with your performance, and I would like to discuss them with you."

"I have noticed that you are not performing up to our expectations. This is not acceptable, and we need to discuss the issue."

"I would like to discuss a few issues that I have noticed regarding your performance. These are the issues."

Final Tips

You should always maintain professionalism when discussing the issues with the employee.

Make sure that you do not lose your temper and be rude to the employee during the discussion.

Always give reasons for why you are discussing issues with the employee.

80. An Employee is Not Reaching Their Potential

Managers are responsible for ensuring that their team is fully optimized and for being the ones to coach their employees to reach their potential. If an employee is not meeting their potential in your opinion, you must be willing to have a difficult conversation with them about it.

Best Approach

This is a tough approach because it forces you to confront an individual on their performance and how they can improve. You want to keep this conversation as productive as possible, so you can both move forward positively.

You must be direct in your approach and have a goal for the conversation. You want the employee to reach their potential so they can add value to your team, but you also want them to improve from a personal standpoint. People get better at their job when they also get to be a better person.

When to Approach

The best time to approach an employee is when you know they are going to be receptive. If you are going to give an employee feedback on their performance, make sure they aren't in the middle of something. You want them to be able to focus on the conversation and put their full attention into it.

What to Say

"I wanted to talk with you about an important topic. I'm concerned that you are not reaching your potential."

"When I look at your duties and what you do for the company, I see there is a lot that needs to be done. You can do so much more."

"I want you to know that I've been looking at your work and I believe you have the potential to be much more productive."

"I've been considering how we can get you to reach your true potential. I think there are a few ways that we can do this. The first thing I want to discuss is your work schedule."

Final Tips

You must be willing to have difficult conversations. If you are afraid to be direct with your employees, then you will never get them to improve or reach their potential.

The goal of this conversation is to have your employee improve their performance and reach their true potential, not necessarily to get them fired. You want them to succeed so the company succeeds, but if they are not meeting their obligations, you need to call them out on it before it gets worse.

Crisis Management

Managers and leaders need to be prepared for the unexpected, which is a given in the workplace. Being prepared and knowing how to handle a crisis is crucial to maintaining a positive reputation as a leader.

81. Death in the Workplace

Death in the workplace is a very sensitive topic. It is highly recommended by company management to handle this issue with great care and concern.

Whether you are a company owner or a manager, you should be well aware of the legal requirements and what actions should be taken in case of a death at the workplace.

Best Approach

Discuss with all the employees in a group and not individually. Confirm the employees' relationship with the deceased. Agree with the other employees to support each other in this difficult time.

Do not force anyone to share his or her feelings immediately. If they are comfortable, let them share their views and concerns. Inform them that they may leave work early if they wish to do so.

Give a detailed account of what has happened giving an unbiased version of events without any blame. This will help your employees to accept the situation and cope with it better.

When to Approach

It is best to approach the topic when you feel that the employees are ready to discuss the matter. It is not a good strategy to confront an employee with this topic when he or she is still in a state of shock.

What to Say

"The death of a person is always a shock and I know it is very difficult to accept. I will be here to support you whenever you are ready to discuss it."

"I know it is very difficult to talk about this. If you would like to discuss it, please let me know."

"I am here to listen to you if you would like to talk about it."

Final Tips

Never try to avoid the topic.

Never dismiss an employee's feelings on this issue.

Make sure you are well informed about the legal requirements in this matter and act accordingly.

82. Malfeasance or Nonfeasance

It would be naïve to assume that employees will always act in the best interests of the organization. All organizations face the reality of nonfeasance and malfeasance, which may result in significant harm to the organization or its members. Nonfeasance is a failure to act which results in harm, whereas malfeasance is a purposeful action which causes harm.

Best Approach

When dealing with nonfeasance or malfeasance, it is best to approach the situation with an open mind. The person who reported the situation may be wrong and may have misunderstood the situation. The person could also be right. The most important thing is to gather as much information about the situation as possible before making any judgments. This will help you decide what course of action to take, and what information you need to collect next.

When to Approach

If you have discovered malfeasance or nonfeasance, you must act immediately. Delays in reprimanding will only make the situation worse and may cause suspicion that you are covering up for the employee. If you have to wait a certain amount of time before acting, ensure that your employee's superiors know they report to you, and explain the situation to them.

What to Say

"I'm concerned about the allegations you have made, and I would like to take a few minutes to discuss the situation with you. Would you like to meet in my office, or would you prefer to talk over a cup of coffee?"

Final Tips

Be consistent in your disciplinary actions. If you are going to reprimand someone for a certain reason, don't make exceptions for anyone else.

Do not reprimand an employee for one instance of nonfeasance or malfeasance without investigating the situation and the employee's history.

83. Undue Influence by a Third Party (a Vendor, Client, or Consultant) on an Employee

According to organizational behavior, undue influence in organizations refers to the excessive social influence from a third party that disrupts or violates the principles of fairness, equality, and justice. In legal terms, undue influence is a term that describes an improper or illegal pressure brought to bear on a person who stands in a fiduciary relationship with another person, especially an elderly or vulnerable person.

Best Approach

When employees are influenced by external factors, the organization can be vulnerable to fraud, loss of intellectual property and confidential information, and reduced employee health and safety. This could result in unfair treatment for an employee who is unable to resist undue influence or pressure from a third party.

When to Approach

When a manager is aware of the undue influence from an external source, it is necessary to discuss with the employee to find out what caused the undue influence.

What to Say

"I have noticed some changes in your behavior lately. Do you feel like someone has put undue influence on you?"

"Have you been approached to do something that is against the organization's policy or your job description?"

Final Tips

A manager should discuss the concerns with the employee in private. Make sure that the employee agrees to be open and honest about the situation. It is also important to collect evidence of undue influence that the manager needs to handle the conversation with the employee.

84. Press Leaks

In the event of an employee making a mistake, providing incorrect information to the media, or leaking company information, it is important for a manager to handle this specific situation in a very delicate manner. Managers should be aware that employees will be more likely to accept a negative situation if the manager goes about it correctly.

Best Approach

A manager must address the issue with employees while remaining as calm as possible. This is important because being angry or upset will make the situation worse and may cause the employee to become more defensive. It would also be a good idea for a manager to speak privately with an employee about the necessary information instead of chastising them in front of other coworkers. This will give the employee a chance to respond calmly and logically, instead of getting defensive from an attack by other coworkers.

When to Approach

You must not wait too long to approach the employee about the information leaked. The longer it takes, the more it will seem like the company is trying to hide something, which can cause other employees to become suspicious as well and may eventually lead to an even larger problem. It is also important for a manager to ensure that they are approaching an employee who is communicating with the media in a professional manner, as well as that they have a professional and clear communication channel with them.

What to Say

"I am concerned that you gave the media incorrect information. When speaking with the media, it is important that you are honest and truthful."

Final Tips

A manager should take the time to discuss the main issue with the employee without going into too much detail. The manager should also be prepared for any questions or concerns that an employee may have regarding the situation. A manager needs to treat the conversation as a solution and not as an attack on an employee.

85. Commercial Espionage

The topic of commercial espionage is not a pleasant one. However, it is an issue that many companies must deal with. This is an issue that is hard to avoid because the information obtained in this way can be highly damaging and costly to the company.

Best Approach

The first step in handling this situation is to talk with the employee about the issue. This will give them a chance to explain what happened. They may be able to justify their actions or give you a reason why they did it. This can help you decide what punishment would be appropriate. Consider talking with a lawyer before doing this so you are fully informed on your legal rights and responsibilities in this situation.

When to Approach

This is a conversation that should be held as soon as possible. The longer you wait, the more damage can be done. A good time to approach the employee is when you have some free time and can make it clear that you are serious about this conversation. You don't want an employee to think they can avoid this problem by waiting until it goes away or by making excuses for their behavior. The best time to talk about this issue is after you have already discussed the situation with your lawyer or other appropriate personnel.

What to Say

"We have received information that you have been taking work home with you, and that you were using your personal computer for this purpose. We are very concerned about this information, and we need to ask you some questions."

"I am concerned that the information may be used for the benefit of a competitor. I'm sure you understand how serious this is and how much damage it could cause to our company."

"Is there anything that you want to tell me about this situation? Have you done anything else that would be important for me to know?"

Final Tips

If the employee admits to committing commercial espionage, you can take appropriate action. If they insist that they did not commit the act, you will probably want to speak with a lawyer about your legal options.

There are laws that protect companies from employees stealing information. You may be able to sue them for monetary damages and other costs that are caused by their behavior.

86. Leaking of Customer Data

The employee has just been caught disclosing customer data. You must handle the situation and the employee properly.

Best Approach

First, give the employee a chance to explain how it happened. Then, discuss the steps that you will take to ensure that it does not happen again. Finally, talk about each of the consequences if it does happen again.

When to Approach

Handle the conversation as soon as possible after the issue has been brought to your attention.

What to Say

"I received a tip that you were selling customer data. Can you explain what happened?"

"I'm very disappointed about the incident. The problem is that customers' privacy is very important to us." (Do not emphasize the word "was" in this sentence, because it may suggest that the employee did not know about it before.)

"So, what happened? Can you tell me how it happened?"

Final Tips

Explain that the employee is responsible for the company's reputation, and that he or she must take it seriously.

Discuss what steps you will take to ensure that it does not happen again. If appropriate, mention some of the consequences if it does.

Avoid any discussions of why the employee did this because it could lead to a discussion of personal matters.

87. Employee's Criminal Action

In most cases, it is difficult to have a conversation with an employee when you are aware that the employee has committed a criminal act. In this case, it will not be easy even if the employee has committed some minor crime. When the crime committed by an employee is serious, you will find it very difficult to have a conversation with him or her.

Best Approach

You are required to discuss the matter in private. You are required to explain why you are having the discussion and should also explain your feelings about the matter. You should try to keep the tone of your voice as neutral as possible and avoid any offensive or belittling comments.

When to Approach

In case you find out that an employee has committed a crime, you should speak to the person as soon as possible. The employee should be given time to understand his or her actions and any consequences of those actions.

What to Say

"I am aware that you have committed a crime. I know that you are aware of the same. I would like to discuss the matter with you in private."

Final Tips

When you are having a conversation with an employee regarding the crime committed by him or her, you should be very careful about not reacting in a manner which can make the person feel offended. You should avoid using any offensive or belittling comments when you are talking to the employee. Also, do not raise your voice against the employee.

88. Civil Complaint of Employee's Behavior in Public

Today's employees are not only the members of the company but also its ambassadors. They represent the company in every interaction they have with the clients and customers. As such, they should always be on their best behavior. However, many times, even an employee who is not on a business trip can get into an altercation with a client or customer and get into an unpleasant situation. Most employees do not know how to handle such situations and end up complicating matters for themselves and the company.

Best Approach

The best approach to discuss such situations with an employee is to have a calm and collected discussion about the issue. The first step is to listen to the employee's version of the story. If possible, get a detailed account of the incident. Once you are clear about what happened, you can proceed further with the discussion.

When to Approach

The employee should be approached as soon as possible after he or she returns from the trip. This is because the employee may want to discuss the incident further, and you can take immediate action.

What to Say

"I'm glad that you told me about this situation. Please talk to me about the entire incident. I want to know your side of the story."

"Tell me what happened."

"Why don't you start from the beginning?"

"What happened before this incident?"

Final Tips

Once you have an idea of what happened, try to understand the reason behind the employee's behavior. You can discuss this with him or her. If you think that there is a cultural difference involved, do not overlook it. It is very important not to jump to conclusions about the employee's action. Also, do not accuse the employee of doing something wrong until you are sure that he or she did something wrong.

89. Release of Leaked Information to Public

The employees' capacity to maintain confidentiality is something that can be severely endangered by the information they have. This can be seen in the case of an employee who is aware of a leak of confidential information, and who shares this information with others. This is also referred to as "information security," which refers to the measures taken by an organization to protect its data from outside access.

Best Approach

A manager should not only know how to discuss the matter with employees, but also have the right approach. The approach should be calm, collected, and considerate of the employee's feelings. This is because the employee may feel as though he or she has done something wrong.

When to Approach

It is best to discuss the matter when it is fresh. Do not leave it for a later time, as this can lead to further issues. If you allow the employee to continue with his or her job, you will be able to find out if he or she has acted on the information received.

What to Say

"I want to talk to you about this information security leak. I know that you have been receiving quite a few calls from the media, but this is something we must take seriously."

"I understand that you are concerned about the well-being of the company, but it is not your job to release information to the public. This is something that can affect our image and your job as well."

"As a result of this leak, I am beginning an investigation. I will be asking you some questions regarding what all has been shared with people outside the organization."

Final Tips

Always conduct the meeting in a private setting and have a member of the Human Resources department present. This will ensure that the employee is treated fairly and given a chance to defend himself or herself.

After the meeting, you should follow up with an email or letter stating the outcome of your investigation. If it is found that the employee has acted irresponsibly, make sure he or she has his or her job terminated with immediate effect.

Morale and Communication

Having a good team is one thing, but ensuring that your team members are happy and are performing to their fullest potential is another. If you are the type of manager who cares for your employees, then you will be able to tell if they are happy and content.

In this chapter, we will discuss how to deal with morale issues, and the most common ways a manager can improve employee morale. We will also discuss several ideas on how to communicate better with your employees.

90. Doesn't Get Along with Others but is Good at His/her Job

A lot of employees do not get along with others in the workplace. They may have some interpersonal issues, or they may just not like people. Regardless of the reasons, this employee does not get along with others and, as a result, is an irritant to everyone.

Best Approach

When dealing with this difficult situation, you can ask the employee how he feels. If the employee does not like working with others, then he should be honest with you. He may be able to suggest some strategies for him to work better with others. You can also try to talk to him about ways he can make his coworkers feel more comfortable around him and how he could do things differently when working in a team environment.

When to Approach

This discussion needs to occur when you notice the employee taking a different approach or working with others in a different way. It is important that you discuss this with him as soon as possible.

What to Say

"I want to have a talk with you about the way you work with others. I have noticed that you do not seem to like working with others and that, as a result, you are not getting along with anyone in the office. As long as you are working here, I feel that you should be getting along with everyone around you. What is it about other people that makes it difficult for you to work together? Do they say anything to upset or offend you? If so, tell me what these things are, and I will help resolve them."

Final Tips

You should not keep this a secret. Eventually other employees will notice that you are dealing with this problem and they will ask you about it. You do not want to tell them that your employee does not get along with others, but you can tell them that you are having problems communicating and working together.

If the employee continues to be a problem after talking with him about the issue, then it may be time for you to terminate his employment. Having an employee who is so disruptive and does not get along with anyone is going to cause problems for your entire staff. It is best if all of your employees can work well together and have a good relationship with each other.

91. Disgruntled Coworker who Loves to Spread Rumors

You must have come across the situation where one of your employees is spreading rumors about coworkers and causing discontent among them. This is a very difficult situation to be in as both these employees are your team members.

Even if you try to ignore the issue, it will keep getting worse and will ultimately affect your business. You must resolve this issue as soon as possible.

Best Approach

In a situation like this, it's best to have a meeting with all your team members. You can also make sure you have the HR department available as well.

During the meeting, you should try to keep your emotions in check and try to be as neutral as possible. You should also take notes to address the issue properly and in detail.

When to Approach

You should approach this situation as soon as possible. The longer you delay the issue, the worse it will get. It is best to resolve it immediately.

What to Say

"I have been informed by a few team members that you have been spreading rumors about others. I strongly believe that you do not want to hurt your colleagues, and this is just an issue of misunderstanding. I would like to hear your side of the story."

Final Tips

The best way to approach this situation is to be as neutral as possible. It's also best to keep your emotions in check so that you can have a clear head and discuss it properly.

92. Rude Coworker Who Doesn't Care About the Team

You have a new employee that just isn't fitting in with the team, and he/she is really bringing down the productivity of your entire department, team, and for that matter, your entire company. You have already talked to him about it, but he/she doesn't seem to care, and because it has been going on for so long, you are not sure what else to say or do.

He/she is always late for meetings, doesn't follow through on assignments and projects, and it seems like he/she just isn't a good fit for the team or the company. It has gone on long enough that it is becoming clear that this employee is not working out and needs to be replaced as soon as possible.

Best Approach

The best way to handle this situation is to talk with the employee about how his/her behavior and attitude toward the team and the work he/she is doing are not working out for him or the company.

It may be that he/she is just not a good fit for this job or the company at this time, and it may be in his/her best interest to find another position where he/she will be able to better fit in.

When to Approach

You should approach this situation as soon as possible, because it is affecting not only the performance of your team and the company, but is also making you and the rest of your team stressed out.

What to Say

"I don't think that you are a good fit for the position or the team. You have been late to meetings, assignments, and projects. It seems that you are not a good fit for this job or the company. I would like to recommend you find another position where you may be better suited."

Final Tips

This is a difficult conversation to have with your employee and it may be tough to face them after you tell them this. But it is important to do so because it is not fair for your company or the team if they are not happy with their job.

93. Meeting Cancellation that Makes the Department Look Bad

If a manager has employees who often miss meetings (without an acceptable reason), it is possible that the manager may have to have a difficult conversation with them about their attendance. This is a difficult conversation because the manager cannot be certain when the employee will return to work after a meeting is canceled or delayed.

Best Approach

To have a productive conversation with employees about meeting cancellation, the manager should take time to think about what they want to communicate. The manager should ask themselves specific questions. Are there times when the employee has good reasons for missing meetings?

When to Approach

The manager should consider when they are most likely to have a productive conversation with an employee about meeting cancellation. For example, the manager should consider that the employee may not be in a good mood or have time to focus on their needs and concerns unless they are contacted early in the day.

What to Say

"I want to talk with you about how often you are missing meetings. You were absent from a meeting that was important to our department, and I am concerned. I need to know that when meetings are important to the department, you will show up for them. The behavior of you being absent from a meeting is unprofessional, and it causes the department to look bad."

Final Tips

The manager should allow for some time (at least a few minutes) for the employee to respond. If the employee is not willing to talk about their attendance, then the manager should still share their concerns and their need for the behavior to change.

The conversation should be handled in a private area at work that is away from distractions and other people who can overhear what is being said.

94. Tries to Take Over a Project that's Not His or Her Responsibility

This is often a common conversation a manager has to have with an employee.

The employee's behavior and approach have compromised the team's ability to get the project done and risk of missing the deadline is high. If you don't take action, you will likely lose your reputation as a manager who can lead a team.

Best Approach

First, make sure the employee's behavior is really putting the team's success at risk. Make sure you have documented proof of his or her actions and/or attitude that shows he or she is not completing his or her responsibilities, failing to follow the team's process, and not meeting project deadlines.

When to Approach

When the employee is not meeting his or her responsibilities on the project, or if you have documented proof that he or she is failing to meet project deadlines and not completing his or her responsibilities.

What to Say

"I've noticed that you haven't been meeting your responsibilities on this project. Instead of pointing fingers, I want to understand your perspective on what we've been doing and what we need to do differently. Does that sound OK with you?"

Final Tips

If the employee's behavior is truly putting the team's success at risk, you may not be able to resolve the issue without taking some form of punitive action. If that seems like your only option, make sure to document all the employee's behaviors that have hurt project success. Then, when you need to have a performance review with him or her, make sure the documented proof is ready for when you need to argue your case.

95. Overly Competitive Coworker

When a coworker becomes overly competitive attempting to get ahead at the expense of other coworkers, it can cause issues in the workplace, and unless you handle it properly, it may even affect your own career.

Best Approach

In discussing this issue with your employee, you need to be very careful. You don't want to make them feel like they are being accused of something, and in fact, that is not the case. You are not accusing them of being overly competitive at all.

When to Approach

In approaching this issue, you want to be as subtle as possible. You want to address it when the employee is not in a competitive situation. You don't want them to feel like you are trying to catch them in the act of being overly competitive.

What to Say

"I would like to have a conversation with you about your coworker. I want to discuss how she is acting toward you."

"You may be aware that she has been overly competitive at work toward you. She may have even made remarks to other coworkers about how she is trying to get ahead of you in the workplace."

"This can certainly create some issues within the workplace, and it makes me feel uncomfortable as your manager. I don't want you to feel like you are being targeted in any way, and I want to make sure that this behavior is not affecting your work performance."

Final Tips

This is a conversation that you should never have with your employee in front of the coworker who is being overly competitive. You don't want to draw any attention toward the situation.

This conversation can be uncomfortable for both you and your employee, so make sure that you are ready for the discussion before approaching it. And when approaching this issue, be sure to be as sensitive as possible while still getting your point across.

96. Lack of Motivation

Engaging in a difficult conversation with an employee about lack of motivation is not easy. However, the fact is that managers must have difficult conversations with employees about this topic at some point.

While it can be uncomfortable and awkward to talk to employees about lack of motivation, you can do this in a way that allows them to save face and that doesn't damage your relationship with them.

Best Approach

If you have concerns about an employee's lack of motivation, you should ask them to come up with some ideas for how to change the situation. Have them approach the topic as a team problem, rather than a personal one.

When to Approach

You should approach the employee about lack of motivation when you notice that they are not performing well. When you notice a large drop in performance, it is time to talk to them. You should also talk to them if they have been doing a good job, but their performance has dropped.

What to Say

"I have noticed that your performance has dropped lately. What can we do together to turn this around?"

"I have noticed that you have had a drop in productivity over the last few weeks. How can we solve this problem together?"

"I have noticed that you are not performing as well as you were a couple of months ago. What happened?"

Final Tips

Remember that the employee has no idea that you think they are not performing as well. If you let them know that you have noticed a drop in performance, they will be surprised and a bit embarrassed.

If the employee feels like they have performed poorly because of outside circumstances, be sure to take those factors into consideration when working with them on solutions.

Remember that the employee is as responsible for solving this problem as you are. You do not want to let them feel like it is your responsibility to fix it.

As uncomfortable as this conversation may feel at first, it is only going to get more uncomfortable if you do not talk about it now.

Conflicts in the Workplace

Employee conflicts happen in all work environments. Most work environments have a person or group of people who create conflict at one point or another.

The purpose of this chapter is to discuss the following types of employee conflict.

97. Working Against the Company's Mission and Values

If an employee is working against the company's mission, they are not following the company's values. This is a very difficult conversation to have with your employees. Everybody needs to be on the same page.

Best Approach

Talk to your employee about your concern. Your goal will be to get the employee to see that they are working against the company's mission and values.

When to Approach

This conversation should be approached as soon as possible. If there is an issue, you should talk to the employee right away and try to understand what happened.

What to Say

"I have noticed that you have been doing (insert behavior). I am concerned about this because it is against our mission and values."

"I want to make sure that we are on the same page. What are your thoughts about this?"

"What were you thinking when you did this?"

"How do you feel about what happened?"

"What should we do moving forward?"

Final Tips

If the employee is not willing to change their behavior, you will need to address the employee's behavior with your supervisor.

If it is something that the employee does not have control over, you should ask them what steps they are willing to take to prevent this from happening in the future. If it is something that they feel they have no control over (i.e., a personal issue), then you should help them find resources or ways to deal with it as an employer.

98. The "Backstabbing" Coworker

A manager should be able to handle difficult conversations with employees about the "backstabbing" coworker. This is a common work issue in many organizations and affects employee morale and productivity.

Best Approach

The best approach to having a difficult conversation with employees about a backstabbing coworker is to call a meeting after lunch time. This way the employee won't feel uncomfortable seeing his or her coworker. It should be a private meeting and should not include other employees. The manager should inform the employee about what was shared with him or her. It would help if the employee has an idea about what this meeting is all about before it actually happens. Also, it would help if they had time to think about it. The manager should ask them how they feel and acknowledge how hard it must be for them to experience such a situation at work.

When to Approach

The manager should approach the situation when it happens. Before approaching the situation, it is important to evaluate if it is a good time to approach. If it is not the right time, then wait until later. Also, the manager should approach his or her employee when they have time to talk. For example, even though the employee's work areas may be noisy, if he or she is busy, then this would not be a good time.

What to Say

"So, I heard that you are having a difficult time with a coworker. How are you doing?"

"I am sorry about this situation. I can see how stressed you are about it."

"I have spoken to the other party and he/she is going to stop doing this."

"I feel like it is my job to support you through this period."

"My door is always open for you if you need to talk about it."

Final Tips

The manager should also be aware of the employee's personality. For example, if he or she is an extrovert, then it might be a good idea to discuss the issue with others to get more opinions. However, if he or she is an introvert, then it is best to discuss the issue with just one person.

After the conversation, the manager should follow up with a written communication. This will help keep the conversation on paper for everyone involved and can be used as future reference.

99. The Complaint from an Employee About Another Employee

When an employee complains about another employee, it may be a very difficult conversation for you as the manager.

You need to understand the issues and how to handle the tough conversation.

Best Approach

The best approach to discussing is to understand the issues and try to solve the problem. You can understand the issue by asking the employee about what has happened and what they think about it.

When to Approach

You can approach when the employee comes to you or when you notice that the employee is not doing a good job in their work.

What to Say

"Thank you for telling me about this issue, I really appreciate it."

"I want to understand your point of view, so I can do what is best for the company and you."

"I understand that you are frustrated with this situation. You want me to fix it, but at this time, I don't have a solution. However, I will keep working on it and come up with a solution."

"You can be frustrated, but you shouldn't complain about another employee behind their back. I want you to discuss any issues that you have with this employee directly and not behind their back."

Final Tips

It's important to understand the issue and the situation before you get into the conversation.

Do not try to solve this problem because it could be a complicated issue.

Understand that you don't have a solution yet, but keep working on it until you come up with one.

100. Conflict Between a Supervisor and Employee

In any company, there can be so many reasons for conflict between a supervisor and employee. today we are going to discuss the fundamental causes of conflicts among employees and supervisors. The first thing that we need to take care of is that both the parties should know they are in conflict. If one party remains unaware of the fact, then it will be difficult for them to solve the problem.

Best Approach

When you must discuss a conflict between a supervisor and employee, it is very important that you choose the right time and place. The best time to discuss this issue is in the office or at the table. The reason for this is that employees tend to get angry when they are at home or during any other time.

When to Approach

The best time to approach the employee is when they are in a good mood. They should be happy or in a good phase of their life. The reason for this is that when they are in a bad mood, it will be difficult for them to express their feelings and it will become difficult for the supervisor to take on the responsibility of solving the problem.

What to Say

"I need to talk to you about the way you are treating your coworker."

"I'm sorry, but I need to talk to you about something."

"I know that we have had some differences in the past, but I want to clear the air and make things better."

"I know that we don't see eye to eye on this issue but it's time we tried to resolve our differences over it."

Final Tips

When you have to speak to an employee, it is very important that you know what to say. Always make sure that you don't begin the conversation in a negative way. For example, if you are going to ask them about the way they are treating their coworker, then it is better not to start with, "You have been treating your coworker wrong." The reason for this is that even if they are not treating their coworker wrong, they will feel that they are being blamed and might become defensive.

The way we finish the conversation should be in a positive manner. We should at least try and resolve the issue between them so there are no conflicts between the two of them in the future.

101. Conflict Between Two Employees

During the workday, your manager has received several complaints about a particular team member. Several of her peers, as well as some upper-level managers, have also mentioned that this same person has been exhibiting disruptive behavior. After much deliberation, your manager has decided that he/she must address this issue with the employee.

Best Approach

The best approach to discuss the conflict between two employees is to include both employees in the discussion. Having each employee present should ensure that neither feels they have been singled out. The first step in the discussion is to find out where this conflict originated. Was there a specific incident that caused this conflict? If so, what was it? To prevent similar occurrences from happening again, it is important to discuss this specific incident at length with both employees.

When to Approach

You should approach the conflict between two employees when the problem has reached a point where it can no longer be ignored. You should also try to discuss this issue as soon as possible. Otherwise, you may risk having one employee begin to resent the other. This resentment can then fester and cause additional problems in the workplace.

What to Say

"I have received several complaints about the two of you. It seems you have been at odds with each other for quite some time. I want to know how this conflict started, and I would like both of you to share your perspectives on the matter. Do either of you have any comments on this matter? If so, I'd like to hear them."

Final Tips

During the discussion, try to remain as objective as possible. If you find that an employee is becoming emotional, you should attempt to calm them down. If possible, the conflict between two employees should be resolved quickly and without too much disruption in the workplace.

102. The Complaint from an Employee About a Supervisor

An employee complaint is a serious matter. It may indicate that you have done something wrong and, to correct the situation, you must first understand the complaint. The first step is to listen to the complaint from your employee without interrupting or being defensive.

Best Approach

Here you must be careful. You must listen to the complaint without being defensive. In case you are not sure of the facts of the complaint, ask your employee to clarify. If the employee is not able to tell you what the problem is, this may be an indication that there has been a misunderstanding. In such a situation also, it is good to ask your employee to clarify his feelings and thoughts so that both of you can reach a common understanding of what has happened.

When to Approach

You must approach your employee whenever you are provided with a credible complaint. In case you have any doubt about the facts of the complaint, you should find out and confirm the facts before approaching your employee. Avoid any kind of confrontational situation.

What to Say

"I have received your complaint. How can I help?"

"Can you tell me more about your complaint? Have you had a similar problem with other people?"

"Do you think that the problem will be solved if I do this...? If not, what will solve the problem?"

"What would you like to see happen to resolve this situation?"

"Do you need any help in resolving this situation?"

Final Tips

Avoid being defensive because this will only aggravate the situation.

Listen to your employee without interrupting and clarify your understanding of the complaint. This will help in reaching a solution.

Once you have reached a common understanding, try to reach a mutually acceptable solution. If you are not able to agree on a solution, talk to your supervisor and ask for his assistance in resolving the issue.

Remember that it is important that you always treat everyone in your organization with respect, dignity, and fairness.

103. Discuss A Disagreement with Another Employee

A difficult conversation with an employee about a disagreement with another employee is one that you must have. These conversations are hard, but it is important to have them. You need to get information from employees and resolve problems.

Best Approach

The best approach for this difficult conversation is to ask open-ended questions. Ask questions that cannot be answered with a simple "yes" or "no." These types of questions are less confrontational and will help you to get information out of the employee.

When to Approach

You should approach this difficult conversation when the employee has had a disagreement with another employee. The issue may have been minor, such as someone going to lunch at the same time as someone else, or major, like an accusation of theft.

What to Say

"I have noticed that there has been a dispute between you and another employee. I'd like to hear both sides of what happened."

"I understand that the other employee said (name) took (item) without replacing it but you say that you did replace the item. Can you explain why?"

"I know that this issue is upsetting to you but it's important that we resolve it as soon as possible. I will gather all the information and we will try to resolve this problem together."

Final Tips

It's important to remember that employees may have different perceptions of the same event. Employees can't be expected to agree on everything every time.

When talking with an employee, remember that you are there to gather information and help the employee work through a problem.

104. Physical Violence

Physical violence can be defined as any physical contact that is unwanted or unintended by the other person. This can include hitting, slapping, punching, kicking, screaming at, or spitting on another person.

Physical violence can be caused by several things. It is related to stress, anger, immaturity, poor coping skills, alcohol or drug use, or an inability to deal with differences in people and situations.

Physical violence is NEVER acceptable.

Communication skills can help prevent physical violence. They can also help to diffuse situations that have erupted into physical violence.

Best Approach

When you learn that physical violence has occurred, your concern is with the safety of your employees and the other people involved.

What to Say

"I am very concerned about the safety of you and everyone involved in this incident. I want to make sure that you are safe and that no one else is harmed."

Final Tips

Listen to what the employee has to say. Their account of the event may not match other accounts.

Be respectful of the employee's feelings. When people are stressed, they often feel that others are not listening to them.

Be prepared for an emotional reaction from the employee; they might deny they have done anything wrong or become angry with you.

Don't try to handle this alone. Talk with a trusted colleague or supervisor about how you should handle this situation.

105. Bringing Personal Conflicts into the Workplace

Many employees who feel that they have been wronged, unfairly treated, or not promoted bring their personal problems into the workplace. As a manager, you need to know how to diffuse these situations before they disrupt the company and harm your own working relationship with the employee.

Best Approach

The best approach is to take time to understand the other person's point of view, even if you do not agree with it. Ask how you can help them. Let the employee know that you are available for any suggestions or assistance they may need and that they are not alone in this.

When to Approach

If you become aware of the problem before it becomes a major disruption, you can approach and ask the employee for your assistance in providing any help that they may need.

What to Say

"I've noticed you have become frustrated about the recent promotion process. I don't want to sound like I'm blowing off your concerns, but I know that this is not the first time that you have asked about this. As a manager, it is my responsibility to promote a person who will help the company grow and who will be an asset to the company. If you are worried about being passed over for a promotion, please let me know what your concerns are and how I can help you."

Final Tips

You can also let the employee know that they are more than welcome to ask for help in dealing with their personal problems. If you have an Employee Assistance Program, it may be a good time to suggest that he or she take advantage of the services offered by the company.

Compensation & Salary

This chapter should be used as a checklist for compensation and salary topics. Typically, employees want a raise or to get a promotion, but this is not always the case. Therefore, there are important issues that need to be addressed before discussing compensation and salary.

It is an important conversation because it can establish trust between the employee and manager. This chapter will help managers learn how to handle this difficult conversation with employees without damaging the relationship in the process.

106. Taking Advantage of Company Benefits or Retirement Plans

In many companies, managers are tasked with the responsibility of having difficult conversations regarding taking advantage of company benefits or retirement plans. Companies offer several benefits and retirement plans for employees to take advantage of. Some employees use these benefits to their own personal advantage and abuse the system, putting the company at risk for hundreds or thousands of dollars in penalties.

Best Approach

This is a very delicate conversation because you are talking about an employee's retirement plan or future. You want to make sure that you have all the facts from the company, and that you are not jumping to conclusions.

When to Approach

This is a tricky situation because the company might be reluctant to share information with you, so you will need to approach this conversation when it is appropriate. You should approach this conversation if you have solid evidence that an employee is taking advantage of the retirement plan or benefits system.

When you approach this conversation, make sure that you have all the facts and that you are not jumping to conclusions. You should also investigate other employees who are in the same boat as this employee.

What to Say

"I have noticed that you have made too many contributions to your retirement plan account. I need to know if you have been taking advantage of the company's retirement plan."

"I am concerned about the amount of money you are contributing to your retirement plan. We have a limit on how much money we allow employees to contribute, and I believe that you are contributing more than the limit."

"You are currently spending an excessive amount of money on health insurance and it is costing the company thousands of dollars a year. You will need to lower your health insurance payments if you want to continue receiving benefits."

"I am concerned about how much vacation time you are taking each year, and it is affecting our bottom line. You will need to reduce your vacation time to continue receiving vacation benefits."

"You are currently taking advantage of the company's tuition reimbursement plan, and we have noticed that you are using it for personal reasons. You are required to use the plan for professional development and education."

Final Tips

When addressing these issues, you want to make sure that you have all the facts. You do not want to jump to conclusions, and you don't want to make any accusations. You need to have all the facts before you approach this conversation.

This is also a very delicate conversation because it involves someone's retirement plan or future. You will need to approach this conversation delicately and with care. Make sure that all your facts are correct before approaching this employee to have the difficult conversation.

107. Internet Research Compensation Raise Requests

When a company is doing well and employees are not compensated for their hard work and productivity, the employee may ask for a raise. This conversation can be quite difficult since it is a delicate balance between rewarding good performance while keeping the company profitable.

Best Approach

When a raise is requested, a good manager should always start by thanking the employee for their hard work and contributions to the company. However, if the employee is requesting raises for all employees or a specific group of employees, do not discuss it with that person. Instead, discuss it with the entire group later in a meeting so that everyone has an equal chance to discuss their views.

When to Approach

A good time to approach a conversation about employee raises is after a pay increase has already been given. With this, the employee should be aware that it will not happen again soon. A good time to ask for a raise is when you are not busy and are able to focus on the topic at hand.

What to Say

"I have reviewed your work, and I see that you are doing a great job. I have also seen your requests for raises for other employees and I would like to discuss this with the entire group together."

"We have had a difficult time keeping up with the demands of the economy lately, and I cannot give raises to everyone. However, if we can come up with a way to accomplish this and keep our company profitable, I am open to hearing your ideas."

"I have decided to give a raise to all employees who have been here for a minimum of five years and have not received a raise in the past three years."

"I am afraid that I cannot give you a raise this time around, but I am open to considering your request in the future."

"I am giving you a small raise, since you have only been with us for six months. When you reach your one-year anniversary, I would be willing to discuss the possibility of a larger raise at that time."

Final Tips

When discussing employee raises or bonuses with an employee, always be open to suggestions. This will make the employee feel valued and appreciated as well as help them feel important and included in the decision-making process.

However, when it comes to large company decisions, always be willing to consider other options and views. A good manager should never make decisions without considering all alternatives.

108. Advising an Employee on a Performance Improvement Plan

The employee performance improvement plan is an important part of the job. It allows the manager to help employees improve their performance and to identify what areas need improvement. An employee needs to work with his or her supervisor and put together a plan for improvement.

Best Approach

Discuss the situation with your employees and ask them to improve in certain areas. Make sure that they know you are taking them seriously and what they need to do. You should also ask them how they feel about the situation.

When to Approach

If you have already discussed your concerns and you have given them information on how to improve, then you should approach the employee. Make sure that you discuss this with them when it is a good time for them to talk. You should not approach the employee after a bad day or when they are not in a good mood.

What to Say

"There are some areas that I feel you need to improve on. I have noticed that you have missed some deadlines, and you do not always complete your work on time. We will be putting together a plan for you to improve in these areas and this will be a chance for you to show me what you are capable of. I understand that sometimes this can be difficult, but I want to help make sure things get better. This is something we can work on improving together."

Final Tips

This conversation can be difficult for both you and the employee, but it is important to make sure you are clear about what is expected from the employee. You should also make sure they know that if they do not improve you will have to take further action.

109. Managing a Salary Dispute with Unionized Employees

One of the biggest challenges that a manager must face is handling salary negotiation disputes with unionized employees. In this section, we will discuss some of the common salary disputes that you need to handle as a manager.

The first type of salary dispute is when an employee is not satisfied with their salary and asks for a raise.

The second type of salary dispute is when an employee feels that they are being paid less than their coworkers in similar positions and wants to know why.

The third type of salary dispute is when an employee claims that they are doing the same work as another employee but are getting paid less.

The final type of dispute occurs when employees have received an across-the-board pay raise but want an additional increase for their efforts and/or performance.

Best Approach

Salary negotiation disputes are the most common and difficult employee-manager discussion. The manager must be able to handle these salary negotiation disputes with a positive, problem-solving attitude. Managers should hold these discussions in private, one-on-one meetings at times when the employee is most receptive to hearing management's side of the story. As a professional manager, you must keep your emotions in check and not take this discussion personally. In addition, as a professional manager you must understand what is involved with salary negotiation disputes in unionized environments.

When to Approach

One of the most important considerations for salary negotiation disputes is timing. When you approach your employee with a salary negotiation dispute it is best to do so at a time when they are receptive to hearing what you have to say. Employees can get very upset with the idea of a salary negotiation dispute. It is best to have an open and honest discussion early on in your relationship with an employee, so that both of you know what the other expects from a salary negotiation dispute and how each of you will handle it.

What to Say

"I understand that you are not happy with your salary. You are correct—it is below the range for the position. I have reviewed your performance throughout the past six months and believe that you are an excellent employee who has met all our expectations. In addition to your salary, we offer a variety of other benefits that you may not be aware of. We offer a flexible time off program, holiday pay, company-paid health insurance, and much more."

"I am sure that in your opinion you are doing just as much work as other similar employees in our department who make more than yourself. This is a sensitive issue and one I will need to investigate further before I can respond to any request for a raise."

"I am happy to report that as part of our annual review we have given everyone in the department an across-the-board pay raise. We were able to do this because of increased productivity throughout the department."

"I am pleased to report that based on your excellent performance over the past six months we would like to offer you an additional increase above what we have given everyone else in the department."

Final Tips

Be honest and sincere when discussing salary negotiation disputes.

Be sure to listen carefully to your employee, and be ready to answer questions.

Be confident that you have done everything you can do within your power to give your employee a fair salary for their performance.

When in doubt, check with a senior executive or Human Resources representative for further assistance.

110. When Your Employee's Salary is not Competitive

The employee is a real talent and has been with the company for a while now, but due to your limited budget, the employee's salary is not competitive to what you could get from the outside.

Best Approach

Suggest a raise and see if the employee is open to it. If the employee is not willing to negotiate, discuss why the employee is unhappy with his current salary. You can offer a job promotion or a role change in exchange for higher salary.

When to Approach

It is better to discuss this when the employee has shown interest in his salary. Make sure that you do not approach the employee when you feel that he is underperforming.

What to Say

"John, I have been thinking about your performance and salary for a while now. I find that you are a real talent and have been with the company for a while now. You have done great work but frankly, your salary is not competitive to what you would get from the outside."

"There are few opportunities for other companies, and I do not want to lose you. I was thinking of offering you a raise in exchange for staying with us for another year. What do you think?"

Final Tips

Be honest with the employee. Make sure that you do not speak about another employee's salary to him.

111. Negotiating an Employee's Reduction in Salary or Annual Bonus

At some point in their career, most employees will ask for a raise, promotion, bonus, or other form of compensation. If they do not receive the additional money, or if they do but do not receive it in the manner they requested, then employee morale can be negatively impacted. In addition, if an employee is underperforming and needs to be let go, then a manager may need to inform an employee that his or her position is being eliminated, and that he or she will be let go due to the company downsizing.

Best Approach

There is no right or wrong way to approach an employee who is asking for a raise, a promotion, a bonus, or other compensation. It is important to understand and respect an employee's request for additional money. Keep in mind that many employees do not know what they are worth and need help in figuring this out. If the employee's request is reasonable, then it should be considered seriously along with other factors such as performance, contribution to the company, etc.

When to Approach

A manager should address an employee's request for additional money when they first hear about the employee's request. It is important to discuss the request with the employee early on in the process so that a manager is not caught off guard by an employee's request in a performance review.

What to Say

"I understand that you would like to negotiate an additional $XXX for your annual bonus."

"I would like to discuss your request for additional money with you."
"I would like to hear more about why you feel you deserve more money."
"I would like to discuss why I feel you do not deserve an additional bonus this year."
"Let's talk about what else you could do in order to earn a higher bonus next year."

Final Tips

When negotiating a raise or discussing other forms of compensation with an employee, it is important for the manager to be open and honest about why they do not think the employee deserves additional money. It can be helpful to create a list before meeting with the employee so that you can keep track of what you have discussed.

Cultural and Social Diversity

This is a chapter on cultural and social diversity. There are many things that we consider to be cultural differences. Religion, language, mannerisms, and culture are all examples of differences that we see as cultural. The world is a very diverse place, and it is therefore important that we understand and respect each other's differences.

112. Speaking Foreign Languages at Work

There is a common scenario when a group of employees goes on a business trip or attends a meeting and there is an employee in the group who speaks a foreign language fluently but is not able to translate the information for other employees.

Best Approach

This is a common situation, and there are high chances that you might have encountered the same situation at your workplace. First, make it clear to the employee that you are not on a personal attack but want to address the issue. There have been many times when an employee has come up with a suggestion for making the work environment better and has been discouraged by the senior management.

When to Approach

You must approach the employee at an appropriate time. It is not a good idea to talk about it during the office hours when the person is busy with other tasks. The right time to talk about it will be when they are at home or on a holiday.

What to Say

"I have noticed that you are fluent in another language. I feel that your fluency in the language will be of great help to the other team members as well as yourself if you would agree to talk in the language instead of translating it for them. This will help save time and it will be a great help for the group."

Final Tips

When you discuss with the employee, you will need to make it clear that you are not asking them to translate in a hurry. You want them to take their time and do a good translation. You can also offer the employee some help in improving their skills in that foreign language.

113. Religious Nuances in the Workplace

One of the most difficult, yet necessary, conversations a manager may have with an employee involves religion and health related issues. While it is important to respect the employee and his/her personal beliefs, it is also important to provide them with a safe working environment.

Best Approach

As a manager, it is important to approach the discussion in a nonconfrontational manner. It is very important to discuss the employee's religious beliefs as they relate to his/her performance at work. For example, if an employee has a religious belief that prevents him/her from working overtime or traveling on short notice, there may be some accommodations that can be made to assist their religious beliefs while ensuring that business needs are met.

When to Approach

The discussion should take place in a private meeting in the employee's office. It is important to discuss this issue before the employee has direct contact with customers, vendors, or other employees. This will ensure that the religious conversion is not taken out of context or misunderstood by others.

What to Say

"John, I have noticed that you have been unable to work overtime during the past few weeks. I was wondering: do you have any religious reasons for this?"

Final Tips

Be sure to keep your tone nonconfrontational and empathetic. You can also recommend that the employee make sure any religious restrictions are documented in his/her personnel file. This will allow you or the Human Resources department to be able to accommodate them if necessary.

114. Employees' Religious Activities at Work

The issue of religious activities at work has become increasingly important. Employees who belong to a cultural or religious minority often feel the need to practice their religion in specific ways.

Some employees may feel that they must wear a head covering or a particular uniform, or pray at a certain time. If they are unable to do so, they may feel out of place, unwelcome, or unaccepted. Employees may also have strong feelings about the subject of religious activities.

Some may feel that such activities should not be allowed in the workplace, while others may feel that it is very important to provide a safe place for employees to practice their religion or cultural traditions.

However, if the religious activities interfere with the business or other employees' work, then the employer has every right to step in. For example, if an employee cannot perform his or her job duties because he or she is required to do certain prayers, the employer can demand that the religious activities be performed at home. The bottom line: employees have a right to practice their religion in the workplace, but they must be able to perform their job duties.

Best Approach

The above scenario is a difficult one to navigate, but there are ways to approach this specific topic. As a company, you should have a policy in place stating whether or not the company allows religious activities in the workplace. You should also provide your employees with an overview of your policies and procedures related to religion. If your company does not allow any type of religious activities in the workplace, you should make that clear to your employees. In addition, if your company does not allow interruptions to the workday, you should also make that clear to your employees.

If your company does allow religious activities in the workplace, you should still be sure to emphasize the importance of your employees' ability to perform their job duties. Finally, you should be sure to emphasize the importance of keeping any religious activities separate from work activities.

When to Approach

If an employee's religious activities affect their ability to perform their job duties, then the employer should step in. The discussion should take place during a performance review or during a one-on-one talk.

What to Say

"I understand that you are an observant (religious adherent). So, I want to make sure that you understand company policy on religious activities. Company policy states that you must perform your job duties without any interference from religious activities."

Final Tips

Be sure to use nonconfrontational language to discuss the importance of your employees' ability to perform their job duties and the importance of keeping any religious activities separate from work activities.

115. Religious Garments at Work

In any established firm, employers are recommended to provide reasonable accommodations for employees to practice their religion in the workplace, unless it results in various adverse effects such as financial setbacks, reduced efficiency at work or breaches the rights of other co-workers.

Best Approach

The best approach is to talk with the employee in a friendly and casual manner regarding the current situation. The manager must learn to identify open-minded individuals that would be open to such conversations. Managers can choose to formulate a fair-minded arrangement in accordance with the religious beliefs of employees unless it violates the terms of agreement. If the religious choices of the employee genuinely results in financial difficulties and an unsafe work environment, then the manager is not required to make any form of arrangement for the employee. As such, it would be ideal to present the conversation in the form of advice.

When to Approach

The conversation should be had as soon as a manager notices a decline in overall performance of the employee or notices a hostile environment in the workplace citing reasons regarding the employee's choice of clothing in the workplace.

What to Say

"I would like to discuss your religious garments and what impact they may have on the job. It would be ideal to avoid any distractions or interference in your work".

Final Tips

If a manager feels that the employee is not able to fulfill his or her job duties because of religious garb, the employee must immediately be made aware of the situation, as it could adversely affect their career growth. Employees cannot hope to receive any form of compensation if their religious choices affects their work performance.

116. Religious Symbols in the Workplace

In today's work environment, it is difficult to discern the difference in personal and work-related practices. Employees are not required to remove or hide their religious symbols in the workplace. Certain employers feel that they encourage unprofessional behavior if such symbols are displayed. However, such religious symbols are allowed by law. If an employee wears a religious symbol, they should be made aware of the impact of their actions in the workplace.

Best Approach

If an employee wears a religious symbol, the employer should approach them and initiate the conversation in a friendly manner. As it is a sensitive topic, certain individuals may feel personally attacked by the conversation. The employer should try to be specific about his/her concern and explain why he/she feels that way. Only if the employee's performance is affected must they be made aware of the effects on the workplace.

When to Approach

The employer should discuss this issue with the employee when there is an evident decline in performance due to their beliefs.

What to Say

"I hope that we can discuss the effects of your religious symbol openly and frankly. I know you have every right to wear your religious symbol, but I would like to explain my concerns".

"Some individuals believe it seems unprofessional for an employee to wear religious symbols in the workplace because it may result in confusion regarding whether or not he or she is available for work-related matters."

"I am very tolerant of employees who come to work wearing religious symbols. I would like to make sure you are aware of the situation and would hopefully make accommodations accordingly.

Final Tips

The employer should honor the employee's request to wear religious symbols and allow him/her to continue working for him/her. An employer can't discriminate against the employee for choosing to express themselves, which would result in the form of harassment. However, the employee must ensure that their choices do not contradict with their productivity in the workplace or infringe upon the rights of others.

117. Religious Dress and Cultural Diversity

An employer may have an employee who wears a traditional religious dress, and the employer must make sure that the employee is safe and comfortable at work. Here are some of the ways that you can communicate with your employee about the dress code.

Best Approach

To begin with, you should start the conversation with an open-minded approach. Do not point out to the employee that she or he is violating the dress code of your organization. The employee may feel offended and leave you without any solution. You can discuss the issue with her or him by using a soft tone and ask them about their religious beliefs and how they can be accommodated at work.

When to Approach

You should approach the employee when you have enough time to discuss the issue with her or him. You can also plan a meeting with your employee and take along some of your superiors. This will help you to avoid any kind of confusion in the future.

What to Say

"Thank you for coming today. I would like to discuss the dress code of our organization. I want to ensure that you are comfortable and safe at work."

"I understand that you wear a traditional religious dress, and I would like to know how we can make sure that you are safe and comfortable in the workplace."

Final Tips

You should be open-minded and have an engaging conversation with your employee. You should give the employee enough time to explain her or his religious beliefs and how she or he can be accommodated at work. You can also take along some of your superiors as they will be able to understand the situation better.

118. LGBTQ Discrimination

It can be very challenging for an LGBTQ employee to be discriminated against at work. Managers need to understand that discrimination in the workplace is against the law. Even though it may not be intentional, many employees still are made to feel as if they are inferior. Also, there can be numerous adverse effects that occur because of this type of discrimination, such as depression and other issues.

Best Approach

This can be a very difficult conversation for an employee to have. This is because they are revealing information about their personal life that they may not want others to know about. The manager needs to approach this professionally so as not to offend or embarrass the employee.

It is also important to be sensitive toward the employee and make sure that there are no offensive comments made that will further aggravate the situation. The manager must set an example of how employees should be treated and show them that they are not going to be discriminated against at work.

When to Approach

It is important to approach this issue right away. It may be appropriate to have a conversation with the employee after they have made the initial complaint. If this isn't possible, it may be best to schedule a time when you can meet with them in person. Also, it would be best to find someone who is the same gender as the employee. This may make it easier for them to speak freely and avoid any discomfort.

What to Say

"I am very sorry that this has occurred. I want to make sure that this does not continue to happen. What can I do to help you feel more comfortable?"

"I have no tolerance for any type of discrimination in the workplace. Are you ok with talking about what happened and how it has affected you?"

Final Tips

Be professional when approaching this issue. Try to use words that are not offensive and will ensure that the employee feels comfortable throughout the conversation. This will make it easier for them to talk about what has been going on and determine how they can settle this issue. It is important to also make sure that you have a good relationship with the employee before bringing up the issue. They are more likely to open up about their feelings if they trust you and feel comfortable around you.

119. Use of Racial, Ethnic, and Gender Slurs in the Workplace

Racial, ethnic, and gender slurs are common but hurtful and offensive expressions that demean a person's race, ethnicity, or gender. While these slurs are often used in casual settings with friends or family members, they should never be used at work. In fact, most employers have policies prohibiting such language.

Best Approach

It is important that you not let the employee's use of a racial, ethnic, or gender slur distract you from the discussion about the impact of the language on other employees. It may be difficult if you feel personally offended by what is said. You must resist responding to the slur with a counterattack. You must keep your focus on how the behavior is affecting other people in the workplace.

When to Approach

It is important that you take immediate action when a slur is used in the workplace. Not only can the language be offensive to other employees, but it can also be upsetting and distracting to them. If you wait too long, employees may become desensitized to the language.

What to Say

"I want to talk to you about the use of racial slurs in your conversation. I know that you are friends with the person you were talking about, but you need to understand that using words like _____ is inappropriate in the workplace. All of us have different backgrounds and cultures, and we need to be respectful of each other."

Final Tips

If the situation escalates, call for assistance from an HR representative or a manager. In many cases, the employee will be receptive to your concerns and will stop using the language. Do not forget to follow-up with the employee a few days after your conversation.

120. Outing a Transgender Employee

Transgender people face discrimination in a variety of ways, and that discrimination can have serious consequences for them. In some states, some laws protect transgender employees from being fired or otherwise discriminated against by employers, but there are also many areas where legal protection does not exist.

Best Approach

Trying to find a middle ground with an employee who is opposed to having a transgender coworker may not be possible.

A manager should consider carefully whether he or she wants to risk his or her job by actively supporting the rights of transgender employees.

The best approach for handling this difficult conversation with an employee may be to discuss the potential issues and let him or her know that you are willing to discuss the issue further if needed. If the employer has a written policy that prohibits harassment and discrimination, let the employee know that the policy is in place and ask him or her to follow it.

When to Approach

The best time for the manager to approach this difficult conversation is when he or she first learns about a transgender employee.

What to Say

"I know that there are some employees who are opposed to having a transgender employee. I want to let you know that I support the rights of transgender employees."

"I don't want this discussion to interfere with our working relationship, so I want to be sure that we stay on topic here. Please keep any comments about the gender identity of your coworker out of this meeting."

"I realize that this is a difficult issue, and I don't expect you to agree with me on all of it. But I do expect you to follow the company policy on harassment and discrimination."

Final Tips

A manager should also know when not to have this difficult conversation. This difficult conversation should not be held in a public place or front of other employees.

If the employee continues to make harassing comments, the employer should consider counseling or discipline. The employer will have a better chance of winning any lawsuits brought by the employee if he or she has previously discussed the harassment policy and reminded the employee that such conduct is prohibited.

www.ingramcontent.com/pod-product-compliance
Lightning Source LLC
Chambersburg PA
CBHW081818200326
41597CB00023B/4290